The Function of Verb Prefixes in Southwestern Otomí

Summer Institute of Linguistics and
The University of Texas at Arlington
Publications in Linguistics

Publication 115

The Function of Verb Prefixes in Southwestern Otomí

Henrietta Andrews

A Publication of
The Summer Institute of Linguistics
and
The University of Texas at Arlington
1993

Library of Congress Catalog No: 93–060250

ISBN: 0–88312–605–2

ISSN: 1040–0850

Cover sketch and design by Hazel Shorey

Copies of this and other publications of the Summer Institute of Linguistics may be obtained from

International Academic Bookstore
7500 W. Camp Wisdom Road
Dallas, TX 75236

Contents

Preface

Southwestern Otomí includes several mutually intelligible dialects spoken in the State of Mexico—sometimes referred to as Otomí of the State of Mexico (Grimes 1992). These data were gathered during the years 1954–1979 in the town of San Felipe Santiago, where there are nearly 10,000 speakers according to the 1980 census. Studies of a dialect similar to that spoken in San Felipe Santiago have been made in adjacent Temoaya County. Illustrations used in this study are from San Felipe unless otherwise specified.

Early on in the years I lived in San Felipe Santiago, I realized that to understand what was being said to me in Otomí, and especially to be able to speak Otomí, it would be crucial for me to gain an understanding of the verb prefix system. I was for a long time puzzled by the number of homophonous prefixes and combinations of prefixes that occur. As a matter of fact, it only gradually dawned upon me that the phonological pattern CCCV was generally the realization of three prefixes and not just one, and that the three had collapsed phonologically from three underlying CV syllables to a single, more complex one. In a word, this study attempts to elucidate my findings over the years on this matter.

The study is based on an analysis of a generous corpus of narrative text, a smaller corpus of expository text, and many sentences which are fragments of conversations with language associates. Sentences recorded from conversations were frequently spoken in response to questions I had concerning other unrecorded sentences. They are included because they provide many illustrations of the function of prefixes.

I am greatly indebted to my friend and colleague, Doris Bartholomew, for making available to me a generous number of texts which she had collected, for keyboarding them along with texts that I had collected, and for arranging that a computer printout of them, accompanied by a concordance, be made. Bartholomew has also studied the verb prefix system and our analyses have much in common.

The following individuals gave texts which are included in the database for this study: Mónico Zamora, Cirilo Aguilar, Rafael Flores, Rita de Morales, Trinidad de Morales, Domingo Sánchez, Juana Escalona de Ordóñez, and Sabina Pimeño de Morales. In addition, shorter pieces of text, many of which are fragments of conversation, are included and come from several sources. During the many years in which I studied the Otomí dialect of San Felipe Santiago, the person with whom I have studied most frequently was Sabina Pimeño de Morales. I am grateful for the friendship and the kindnesses of all these friends.

References

Andrews, Henrietta. 1949. Phonemes and morphophonemes of Temoayan Otomí. International Journal of American Linguistics 15:213–22.

———. 1955. Otomí place-names in the State of México. Revista Mexicana de Estudios Antropológicos 14:161–64.

———. 1972. Rhetorical questions in Otomí of the State of México (San Felipe Santiago). Notes on Translation 44:25–28.

Anon. 1893. Luces del otomí. México: Eustaquio Buelna.

Bartholomew, Doris A. 1954–55. Palabras prestadas del español en el dialecto otomí. Revista Mexicana de Estudios Antropológicos 14:169–71.

———. 1960. Some revisions of Proto-Otomí consonants. International Journal of Américan Linguistics 26:317–29.

Cárceres, Pedro de. 1907. Arte de la lengua otomí. In Nicolás de León (ed.), Boletín del Instituto Bibliográfico Mexicano 6:39–155.

Comrie, Bernard. 1976. Aspect: An introduction to the study of verbal aspect and related problems. Cambridge: Cambridge University Press.

Grimes, Joseph E. 1975. The thread of discourse. The Hague: Mouton.

Grimes, Barbara F., ed. 1992. Ethnologue: Languages of the world, twelfth edition. Dallas: Summer Institute of Linguistics.

Lanier, Nancy. 1968. Three structural layers in Mezquital Otomí clauses. Linguistics 43:32–85.

Longacre, Robert E. 1976. An anatomy of speech notions. Lisse: de Ridder.

Newman, Stanley and Robert Weitlaner. 1950. Central Otomían I: Proto-Otomí reconstructions. International Journal of American Linguistics 16:1–19.

Payne, Thomas E. 1989. Medial clauses and interclausal relations in Panare. ms.

Sinclair, Donald and Kenneth L. Pike. 1948. The tonemes of Mezquital Otomí. International Journal of American Linguistics 14:91–98.

Abbreviations

The following abbreviations are used throughout this study. Some of them combine with others to represent a combination of meaning parameters associated with a single form, as in NEG! (negative imperative) and ccs3 (centric singular third-person). In the case of verb prefixes with complex semantic reference, the several parts of a combination of abbreviations are usually separated by ligatures in the hope that this will make for easier reading, as in SQ^xc^2 (sequential excentric second person).

!	imperative	I	incompletive
?	interrogative	IMPF	imperfect
1	first person	in	indefinite
2	second person	IR, ir	irrealis
3	third person	NEG	negative
AFF	affirmation	p	plural
ANA	anaphoric	P	present
BEN	benefactive	PASS	passive
C	completive	PNC	punctiliar
cc	centric	PR	previous
cc_1	$centric_1$	PRG	progressive
cc_2	$centric_2$	REFL	reflexive
d	dual	REL	relative word
df	definite	s	singular
DUR	durative	SM	simultaneous
EL	eventline	ST	stative
EMPH	emphasis	SQ	sequential
F	future	x	exclusive
FP	future perfect	xc	excentric
i	inclusive		

1
Introduction

The verb in Southwestern Otomí is normally preceded by from one to three prefixes which pertain to a complex inflectional system for marking person-of-subject, the time of the action, its location (or direction, in the case of motion verbs), aspect, and mode. In addition, certain prefixes mark clauses which constitute the eventline in narrative text or the principal assertion in a conversation or exposition. The purpose of this study is to show how verb prefixes function in the Otomí sentence.[1]

[1]The phonemes of the San Felipe Santiago dialect are *p t c č k ʔ b d z ž g s š h m n ñ l r w y i ɨ u e ə o æ a ɔ į ų ę ą*. The tones are high (á), low (à), and rising (ǎ) on root syllables and high and low on prefixes. Tone is not contrastive on suffixes. It is here omitted on most Spanish borrowings as well as from words on which it was not recorded in the field. Stress is normally not written but occurs on the first syllable of a verb root and is indicated in this study by a vertical stroke (ˈ) when verb prefixes are present. Morphemes are here generally separated by hyphen (-), except in the case of the last of a string of one or more inflectional prefixes, which is separated from a following derivational prefix or root by double hyphen (=). The phonemic system of San Felipe Santiago is almost the same as that of the Temoaya dialect described in Andrews 1949. San Felipe has nasalized *ę*, which is lacking in Temoaya. In this language, and all other Otomí dialects spoken in the State of Mexico, verb stems ending with certain syllables or *y* lose these endings in utterance-medial position. For instance, *bì=ˈthogi* 'he passed by' becomes *bì=ˈthoh nɨ* 'he passed by there' when *nɨ* 'there' is added. The lost element of such stems is replaced by *h* or *ʔ*, depending upon the first consonant of the word that follows. Such apocope is represented by *H*, whether actualizing as *h* or *ʔ*.

The three orders of verb prefixes are presented in §§3–6. Before these are addressed, however, a number of preliminary matters need to be discussed. This first introductory chapter deals with most of these:

§1.1 the concept of DEIXIS as it relates to this study,
§1.2 the DEICTIC CENTER as it relates to deictic reference,
§1.3 the conditions under which a verb may occasionally occur without a prefix,
§1.4 the deictic adverbs of Otomí,
§1.5 the directional suffixes specific to motion verbs,
§1.6 derivational verb prefixes in relation to the inflectional prefixes under attention here,
§1.7 the phonological reduction of prefixes which precipitates some of the difficulties inherent in the analysis of their form and use,
§1.8 phonological processes associated with some prefixes which add features to (= augment) certain verb roots which follow them, and
§1.9 contextual means for reducing ambiguity when prefix strings are homophonous.

A second preliminary chapter follows this one to deal with the structure of the Otomí noun phrase, since deictic reference in nominals needs to be understood for the reader to be able to adequately evaluate the Otomí sentences provided to illustrate the uses of verb prefixes.

After these preliminaries, the prefixes themselves are presented in the remaining four chapters of the study. An extended Otomí sample of text is then provided at the end of the volume to further illustrate the language.

1.1. Deixis in Otomí. A key element to understanding the makeup of Otomí verbs is the role of deixis both in the verb itself and elsewhere in the sentence. Every independent sentence in Otomí is grounded in reality through deixis, and every dependent sentence DEPENDS upon deictic grounding in sentences around it. Deictic categories are marked in the clause in a variety of ways and, in my experience, attempting to elicit Otomí paradigmatic material out of context is almost impossible because of a need to know the temporal and spatial setting of an utterance before it can properly be produced.

Many verb prefixes encode this sort of information and must often be in concordance with deictic pronouns, noun determiners, certain verb suffixes, or deictic adverbs that occur in the context, especially within the same clause or sentence. In (1), for example, centric prefixes on two successive verbs concord with centric adverbs. The first future-centric prefix places the addressee near the speaker. The first centric$_2$ adverb directs the addressee to look some distance from the speaker's location to a place referenced concordantly by a second occurrence of the centric$_2$ adverb which references the location of the unnamed subject of the second verb. The second verb has two prefixes. The first one, third-person present tense, has no deictic force. The second one places the subject of the verb within view, approximately at eye-level.

(1) *y= ˈthí nɨ̀, Ø-rá= ˈʔyŏ nɨ̀ hâr hwą́h*
F^cc^2=look cc$_2$ P^3-PNC^cc=ˈwalk cc$_2$ at^s field
Look there! It is walking there in the field.

In (2), there are three deictic references. The sentence begins with a topic noun phrase with a centric$_2$ determiner, which locates the addressee's pet dog somewhat distant from the speaker but within sight. Moving past the verb to the second noun phrase, the excentric determiner locates the speaker's dog (which he owns jointly with other persons) out of sight. Finally, the verb has a future-centric prefix (centric$_1$ and centric$_2$ not being distinguished), which implies the speaker's dog will come to a location near the speaker and addressee where it will bite the addressee's dog.

(2) *nìr cí ʔyó, dà$_v$= ˈzà kàm ʔyó-gɔ-he yá*
ccs2 pet dog F^cc^3=bite xcs1 dog-1-px now
Your pet dog, our dog will bite it!

Payne (1989) asserts generally that an event is grounded in reality by the encoding of four deictic operations and that grounded events are encoded in independent clauses. This accords with my findings for Southwestern Otomí, where clauses which carry the eventline in narrative and the principal assertions in exposition are independent clauses. There are a few cases in conversation in which a dependent clause functions as a sentence, but the principal assertions of conversation are also encoded as independent clauses.

Following Grimes 1975 and Longacre 1976, I define an event as that which is encoded by a piece of 'foreground' information in a narrative. Labov and Waletsy (quoted in Payne 1989:4) further define events as "those concepts that take up space on the timeline, i.e., that are temporally ordered with respect to one another, and which cannot be reordered without destroying the continuity of the narration." Thus the eventline is the sequence of clauses which give a step-by-step account of what happened.

The four deictic operations which serve to ground an event or an assertion in reality are: (a) its spatial location (and sometimes direction), (b) the time at which it takes place, (c) the participant reference, which for the Otomí prefix system is the person of the subject, and (d) realis mode, i.e., the actuality of the event or assertion. A clause which encodes these four parameters is completely inflected in Otomí and is thus fully finite and independent.

Payne defines a dependent clause as one which encodes less than these four deictic operations, with the implication that there is an independent clause in the nearby context which grounds the event.

A clause may be independent in the sense of being fully grounded but not be the main clause of a sentence. As will be seen below, it is a second-order primary prefix which encodes the deictic elements that ground a clause and make it independent. Any primary prefix or string of prefixes which includes a primary prefix encodes the four deictic operations needed to constitute the clause as a sentence. Many independent clauses, however, are not the main clauses of the sentences in which they occur. In (3), for example, the first clause is the main clause, but the second, although fully inflected and able to function as a sentence since it includes the same primary, second-order prefix *ʔì-* (third-person present) as the first clause, is in fact embedded within the subject noun phrase as a postposed modifier of the noun.

(3) *ʔì='ʔbɨ̀H yɨ̀ dohto ʔì='hą ɨ̀r reloh*
P^3=be cc₂p doctor P^3=have ins clock
There are doctors who have watches.

Conversely, some clauses which are not fully inflected occur as the only clause of a sentence. Such a clause is dependent upon some other clause in the near context which is fully grounded, i.e., a clause which contains a primary prefix. A clause may thus be the main clause of a sentence but be dependent within the larger discourse. This is illustrated in (4), where the single clause in (4b) has only a conjunct prefix; it is a main clause, but dependent upon (4a), which is also a main clause.

(4) a. *gɔʔtho ší-∅ᵥ='ndù kí bąhci gege*
all EL-C^3=die xcp3 child ANA
All of her children have died.

b. *nim pa ʔnár bąhci š-kán='te*
NEG one^3 one^3 child EL-SM^cc^C^3=mature
Not even one of her children has grown up.

1.2. The deictic center. The DEICTIC CENTER of each piece of text is well marked in Otomí morphosyntactic structure, most clearly articulated by the verb prefix system. It is expressed to a lesser degree by noun determiners, which mark a referent as in-sight or out-of-sight, by deictic pronouns and deictic adverbs which define three degrees of distance from the deictic center, and by motion-verb suffixes which distinguish motion towards the deictic center from motion away from it.

The deictic center of a linguistic exposition is THE LOCATION AND TIME at which the discourse takes place. In the case of narrative, the deictic center indicates the location and time at which the events narrated take place. Distance from the deictic center is categorized in terms of up to three values: CENTRIC_1 (cc_1) is immediately adjacent to the place at which the discourse or narrated events take place, as for instance, an object in the hand of the speaker; CENTRIC_2 (cc_2) is, generally, within sight of the deictic center, whether near or far, but not immediately adjacent to it; EXCENTRIC (xc) is normally out of sight of the deictic center, although the actual distance may be near or far. These three deictic ranges are distinguished in noun determiners, deictic pronouns, and deictic adverbs. Verb prefixes, on the other hand, normally distinguish only two degrees of distance: referencing an action that takes place at the deictic center as CENTRIC (cc) and one which takes place at or from another location as EXCENTRIC (xc).

In narrative, the deictic center for the eventline is usually established by an adverbial clause at or near the beginning of a text. The deictic orientation of a noun phrase, however, is generally determined by the place at which the narrative is spoken. Thus, if an individual who is one of the principals in the narrative is present when it is given, that individual is described as in sight, even though the narrative is in the past tense. For example, the possessive determiner *nìm* (centric_2 singular first-person possessive) and the anaphoric pronoun *ní* (centric_2) in (5) show that the horse referred to in the narrative was near and in view of the deictic center at the time the story was related.

(5) ... *pe* *m-bú='ncų* *ya* *nìm* *phani-he,*
but IMPF-SM^xc^3=fear now $\text{cc}_2\text{s}1$ horse-1x

bú=ndo-'timphani *ya* *ní*
SM^xc^3=greatly-gallop now cc_2

... but he was very much frightened then, our horse; it galloped very fast then.

Another context in which the deictic referent for a noun phrase may be different from that encoded by nearby clauses is that of direct speech in narrative text. The noun phrases in such speeches reflect the deictic viewpoint of the speaker. The determiner ***nɨ̀r*** (centric$_2$ singular) in (6), for example, shows that the document mentioned was in-sight for the speaker (even when it is out-of-sight for those listening to the narrative).

(6) *ʔį̱ną̱, š-tá=ˈmǎ-gɔ ... mismo-gɔ, má co-gɔ nɨ̀r hæʔmi*
say EL-SM^1=go-1 self-1 go leave-1 cc$_2$s document
He says, "I am going to go, I myself, (I'll) go and leave this document (there)."

The first-person speaker is normally considered to be at the deictic center. For a clause to indicate first-person subject at an excentric location, (a) a first-order locational or directional prefix must accompany the second-order subject-encoding prefix, (b) an adverbial clause may encode the excentric location, or both strategies may be employed. Such a situation is illustrated in (7), where *bá-* (progressive completive) implies motion towards the deictic center.

(7) *g-wá=ˈkóhi*
F^1-PRG^C=come^back
I am going to come back.

The deixis of determiners and pronouns is described and illustrated in §2, that of prefixes is described in §§3–6, that of adverbs and verb suffixes follows in this chapter.

1.3. Verbs without prefixes. It is normal for a verb to have at least one prefix; that is, a second-order prefix that marks the subject of the clause as well as tense or aspect and, in some cases, deixis. An irrealis verb is always so marked, but there are a few specific contexts in which, in realis clauses, the subject may lack overt marking in the verb.

For example, a noninitial clause of a sentence which has a sequence of two or more clauses with a primary prefix in simple form in the first clause may lack subject marking when the subject is the same as that marked by the first clause. The quotative morpheme *ʔną́*, which is an abbreviation for *ʔį̱ną̱* 's/he says' and marks direct speech, occurs without an overtly marked subject. Furthermore, the subject may be unmarked in conversation in a clause requiring no other prefix, when the subject is clear from the context.

In the conversational fragment of (8a), the speaker joins an imperative clause and a first-person future clause without overt reference to subjects.

In (8b) and (8c), successive clauses with unmarked subjects encode rapid action or a tense emotional atmosphere. Sentence (8d) is a proverb in which a third-person subject is unmarked in both of its clauses. Sentence (8e) is a sequence of two statements having the same subject and tense-aspect, with the second lacking a prefix.

(8) a. *tə́ʔmi-hmą̣, ma khų̀ti ʔnà thɔ́y*
wait!-just go pay one debt
Just wait a little; I'm going to go and pay a debt.

b. *bìᵥ=ndò-ˈzų̀-hɨ kàr ʔye; sta hwǽci khą̣̀ máfi,*
C^3=great-afraid-p xcs rain EMPH lightning and thunder say

hwǽci khą̣̀ máfi, khą̣̀ rá=ndò-ˈmæ̀šų̌y, ʔną̣́
lightning and thunder and PNC^cc=great-dark say
They were very much afraid of the rainstorm; it really lightninged and thundered, they said, lightninged and thundered, and it was terribly dark, they said.

c. . . . *khą̣̀ kár ʔbæhñą̣ kàr masedonio, ʔyo khą̣̀ zóni, ʔyo khą̣̀*
and xcs3 woman xcs Macedonio walk and weep walk and

zóni
weep
. . . and the wife of Macedonio, she walks and weeps, walks and weeps.

d. *tù khą̣̀ ʔbɨy*
die and born
Some die, and some are born.

e. *dú=ˈma kʔą̣hti-ki-tho-hɨ*
C^1=go see-2-AFF-p
I went and just watched you (pl).

1.4. Deictic adverbs. Three deictic adverbs reference the three locations encoded by noun determiners: *wa* or *kwa* 'here, at or near and in-sight from the deictic center (centric$_1$)', *nɨ* 'over there, a distance from the deictic center and in-sight (centric$_2$)', and *pi* 'there, either near to the deictic center or far away but usually out-of-sight (excentric)'.[2]

Prefixes which have deictic reference agree with deictic adverbs with which they occur within a clause. The three degrees of deictic distance are illustrated by combinations of adverbs and prefixes in (9), (10), and (11), respectively.

(9) a. *ʔă d-rá='hu̜-di wa mbo*
now P^1-PNC^cc=sit-AFF cc_1 inside
I'm just sitting here inside.

b. *dí='ʔdačæ dí='hu̜h kwa*
P^1=alone P^1=sit cc_1
I am sitting here alone.

c. *d-rá='pəš-kwa ∅-bí='kha wa*
P^1-PNC^cc=ascend-cc_1 P^3-PNC^cc=located cc_1
I'm going up here (in sight).)

(10) a. *dú='hanti-ki š-kíy='ka̜H ni*
C^1=see-2 EL-SQ^xc^2=come^down cc_2
I saw you had come down from over there.

b. *hi̜ ∅-rá='ʔwa̜H ni ∅-rá='khă*
NEG P^3-PNC^cc=rain cc_2 P^3-PNC^cc=make cc_2
It isn't raining over there (in sight).

(11) a. *pəH pi rà='kha pi*
place! xc PNC^cc=located xc
Set it down there (on the floor)!

b. *geH pi ∅-rá='kha pi ∅-rá='mphəhni*
be xc P^3-PNC^cc=located xc P^3-PNC^cc=explode
It's over there (out-of-sight) that they (fireworks) are exploding.

c. *ya ∅-ríy='ʔmiH pi hâr zabi pi ∅-ríy=*
now P^3-DUR=live xc at^s pond xc P^3-DUR=located xc
Now she lives over there by the pond, over beyond (the hill).

[2]These adverbs cause the loss of the second-syllable vowel of disyllabic verb stems. Although *pi* is glossed as excentric, it is sometimes used in a nonlocational sense to express an abstraction.

1.5. Directional verb suffixes. A number of verb suffixes occur in Otomí which cannot be described within the scope of this study, although examples of them occur in illustrations that focus on other features. Such suffixes mark person-of-object, nonsingular number, and such matters as emphasis, frustration, and affirmation. But there is one set of suffixes occurring with verbs of motion that needs at least minor mention since they relate action to the deictic center by distinguishing motion towards the deictic center from motion away from it. A number of such verbs and suffixes are listed in (12), but the list is not comprehensive.

(12) *cə-hə* 'arrive at cc_1'
cə-ni 'arrive at cc_2'
cə-te 'arrive at xc'
kɨ-hɨ 'enter at cc_1'
kɨ-ti 'enter at xc'
pə-hə 'exit at cc_1'
pə-ni 'exit from cc_2'
tu̜ 'carry (heavy object) to cc_1'
tu̜-ci 'carry (heavy object) from cc'
kɨ 'carry (light multiple objects) to cc_1'
kɨ-ci 'carry (light multiple objects) from cc'
thæ 'carry (in both hands) to cc_1'
thæ-ci 'carry (in both hands) from cc'
ci-hi 'bring (animate object) to cc_1'
ci-ci 'take (animate object) from cc'
ka̜-ha̜ 'carry (limp object) to cc_1'
ka̜-ci 'carry (limp object) from cc'

1.6. Derivational prefixes. Mention needs also to be made of a limited number of derivational prefixes which differ from the inflectional prefixes which are the primary focus of this study. In particular, there is a small set of adverbial prefixes, here treated as derivational stem formatives which may occur between the verb root and the three orders of inflectional prefixes. The principal members of this class of adverbial prefixes are listed in (13).

(13) *ʔnà-* 'suddenly'
cí- 'slightly'
ndòhta-, ndò- 'greatly'

The forms *cí-* 'slightly' and *ndò-* 'great' may also modify nouns, where they translate as 'small, young' and 'large, old', respectively.

(14) a. *bú=ʔnà-ˈkʔą ya kár macho kí sario*
SM^xc^3=suddenly-appear now xcs3 mule xcp3 Cesario
Then from over there suddenly the mule of Cesario's family appeared (from behind something).

b. . . . *pe kɨ̀ mí-∅=cí-ˈʔəde, mí-∅=ˈkanta-hɨ*
but xcp IMPF-P^3=slightly-understand IMPF-P^3=sing-p
. . . but those who understood a little used to sing.

c. *mí-∅=ndòhta-ˈʔęmę-hɨ kɨ́*
IMPF-P^3=great-believe-p xcp
They used to completely believe in those things.

d. *mí-∅=ˈhoni-hɨ kár cí bą̀hci*
IMPF-P^3=seek-p xcs3 little child
They were looking for their little child.

e. *gege ∅-bà=ndò-ˈtæn kɨ̀ khąʔnį rá-ˈngų*
ANA P^3-PRG^I=great-follow xcp person ST-many
A lot of people are coming, (they are) very much following him.

f. *š-tù=ˈpəš ką́, kàr ndò dą̀hcə kà ∅-rí$_v$=ˈnįgi . . .*
EL-F^xc^3=go^up xcs xcs big planet REL P3-DUR=appear
When it comes up, that one, the big star that appears (over there) . . .

1.7. The phonological reduction of verb prefixes. We are here concerned primarily with the description of verb prefixes. Although almost every prefix discussed in this study may occur in some context as a separate syllable—most typically of CV form with high or low tone—strings of two or three of them invariably reduce to a single syllable when occurring together within a word. Given that the full inventory of verb prefixes makes use of a limited subset of the phonemic inventory presented above, a high degree of homophony results, yielding attendant difficulties for morphological identification. The following discussion lays the groundwork for clarifying issues in identifying which affixes are in fact present when phonological reshaping takes place. We begin by proposing the combinations of underlying forms that actually occur.

First, when two or three prefixes occur together, the vowel and tone of the prefix closest to the stem (the rightmost prefix) are normally retained and other vowels and tones are lost. For example, *gù-* (first-person future) loses its vowel and low tone when followed by *rá-* (punctiliar centric realis, at eye level), as illustrated in (15a), whereas *gí-* (second-person present) loses its vowel and high tone when followed by *dì-* (durative irrealis incompletive), as illustrated in (15b).

(15) a. *ya g-rá='ma pì hár šụmɨy*
now F^1-PNC^cc=go xc at^3 shade
I'm going over there into the shade.

b. *tòhá g-rì='mạ ya ší-∅='thogi*
perhaps P^2-DURir^I=say now EL-P^3=pass
Perhaps you are saying, they have already passed by.

The result of losing vowels and tones, then, is a string of two or three consonants to which a number of phonological processes apply. In one case, where a sequence of two prefixes both begin with *d,* one of the consonants is lost as well. Beginning from the left, the two third-order prefixes begin with the consonants *m* and *š,* respectively. These may be followed directly by second-order prefixes which begin with the consonants *b, d,* or *g,* except in the case of the third-person present-tense prefix which has a zero variant in certain contexts.[3] First-order prefixes may begin with the consonants *b, d,* or *r* and may combine either with second-order prefixes alone or together with both third- and second-order prefixes. Choice of the zero variant of the second-order third-person present-tense prefix results in third-order prefixes effectively occurring adjacent to first-order prefixes as well. Given these facts, the sequences of underlying consonants that could theoretically occur are listed in (16), with sequences which do not actually occur being starred (*). These underlying sequences are actually realized as in (17).

(16)

third + second	third + first	second + first	third + second + first
mb	*mb md mr*	*bb* bd* br**	*mbb* mbd* mbr**
md		*db* dd dr*	*mdb* mdd* mdr*
mg		*gb gd gr*	*mgb mgd mgr*
*šb**	*šb šd šr*		*šbb* šbd* šbr**
šd			*šdb* šdd šdr*
šg			*šgb šgd šgr*

[3]This same morpheme has a third variant which begins with glottal stop; but, since this variant does not combine with other prefixes, it does not figure in the phonological processes discussed here.

(17)

third + second	third + first			second + first			third + second + first		
mb	*mb*	*nd*	*mr*						
nd					*d*	*dr*			*ndr*
ng				*gw*	*gr*	*gr*	*ngw*	*ngr*	*ngr*
	šp	*št*	*šn*						
št								*št*	*štr*
šk							*škw*	*škr*	*škr*

By comparing (16) and (17), we notice four general phonological processes: (a) assimilation of nasal to point of articulation of a following stop, (b) devoicing of stops following *š*, (c) weakening of *b* to *w* and *d* to *r* following *g* and complete loss of *d* following *d,* and (d) nasalization of *r* following *š*.

First, nasal *m* assimilates in point of articulation to a following stop. Underlying *md* becomes *nd;* underlying *mg* becomes *ng* (with subphonemic velar articulation). Resulting forms are illustrated in (18).

(18) a. *m-bú='ncų*
IMPF-SM^xc^3=fear
He was very much frightened.

b. *n-dú='pəhə*
IMPF-C^1=come^out
when I was coming out

c. *n-gú='thæ-wi*
IMPF-C^2=meet-d
when you two met

Second, stops are devoiced following voiceless *š*. Resulting forms are illustrated in (19).

(19) a. *š-∅-pí='cəni*
EL-P^3-PNC^xc=arrive^there
s/he is arriving up there

b. *š-tí='ʔdaʔ-ki*
EL-P^1=give-2
I'm giving it to you

c. *š-kú='kʔąʔti*
EL-C^2=see
you saw it

Third, the voiced stop *b* is weakened to *w* when following the voiced velar stop *g*, as in (20a) and (20b), *d* is weakened to *r* when following *g*, as in (20c), and *d* is lost altogether when following itself, as in (20d).

(20) a. *g-wí='ʔbìh-ke*
P^2-PNC^xc=be-2
you live up here

b. *g-wá='kohi*
F^1-PRG^C=come^back
I am coming back

c. *g-rì='koh-ke*
P^2-DURir^I=return-2
you (customarily) come back

d. *ʔbì dì='ʔbìH kwa*
when F^cc^3^DURir^I=be cc_1
if she is here

A more general statement regarding the context of this weakening is possible, but none of the three first-order prefixes beginning with *b* are attested with any of the numerous second-order prefixes that begin with *b* or *d*. Possible causes for this distributional limitation are as yet unknown although there is another context in which the sequences *dw* and *gw* occur that may ultimately figure in an explanation. Specifically, when the word *hín* (negative) precedes a sequence of prefixes with consonants *m* + *d* or *m* + *g*, the consonants metathesize and *m* is weakened to *w*, yielding *dw* and *gw*, respectively. This phenomenon may have interfered with the weakening of *b* to *w* in some way, but I have no assurance that this is so at this time. The weakening and metathesis of *m* is illustrated in (21).

(21) a. *hín dwí='meya-ki*
NEG IMPF^P^1=know-2
I did not know you

b. *hín gwí= 'ci*
NEG IMPF^P^2=drink
you did not used to drink it

Fourth, *r* becomes *n* following *š*, as illustrated in (22). This can only occur when the zero second-order prefix is chosen.

(22) a. *š-Ø-ní*$_V$*= 'ga̧hki*
EL-P^3-DUR=catch
s/he catches it

b. *š-Ø-nà= 'ʔbəni*
EL-P^3-PNC^ir=lie
it is lying down here

When sequences of three consonants occur, these same processes operate (excluding the last, which can happen with only two consonants present). A few examples of three-consonant sequences are presented in (23).

(23) a. *n-d-rá= 'ʔbɨ̀y*
IMPF-P^1-PNC^cc=be
when I was there

b. *n-g-rá= 'tě̌š*
IMPF-P^2-PNC^cc=mount
you were getting on it

c. *n-g-wí= 'ʔyo-wi*
IMPF-P^2-PNC^xc=walk-d
you two were up (there) walking around

d. *š-t-rá= 'pɔši*
EL-P^1-PNC^cc=wrap
I am about to wrap it up

e. *š-k-rá= 'paši*
EL-P^2-PNC^cc=sweep
you are sweeping

f. *š-k-wá= 'kohi*
EL-F^1-PRG^C=come^back
when I come back

In addition to these four general processes and the exceptions cited above, there are a few other miscellaneous phonological facts that need to be mentioned. The first of these is to explain the absence of the underlying sequence *šb* where *b* has its source in a second-order prefix.

While the underlying sequence *šb* could potentially involve any of three second-order prefixes which begin with *b*, the sequence is only attested with first-order prefixes that begin with *b*. Of the three eligible second-order prefixes, two—*bu*$_y$- (simultaneous excentric second-person) and *bu*- (simultaneous excentric third-person)—are semantically incompatible with *ší*- (eventline). The third second-order prefix *bì*$_v$- (third-person completive) unaccountably results in *ší*$_n$- when combined with *ší*-, with nasal augment ($_n$) as the only trace of the presence of *bì*$_v$-. This is highlighted in (24), where the only difference between (24a) and (24b) is a shift from second-person completive *gú*$_y$- to third-person completive *bì*$_v$-.

(24) a. *š-kú= 'cəhə*
EL-C^2=arrive
you have arrived

b. *ší-*$_n$*= 'nzəhə*
EL-C^3=arrive
s/he has arrived

A second special situation is the sequence of prefixes *mí*- (imperfect) + *bì*$_v$- (third-person completive). While the expected form would be *mbì*$_v$-, the final form in the speech of older speakers is *mí*$_v$, with *mí*- unexpectedly retaining its vowel and tone and the only trace of *bì*$_v$- being the voicing augment ($_v$). Younger speakers tend to drop even the voicing augment and speakers who use *mí*$_v$- frequently omit *ʔbɨ̀* 'when' from temporal clauses. This situation is contrasted in (25a) with that in which the sequence *mb* actually occurs, as in (25b) and (25c).

(25) a. *mí-*$_v$*= 'zɨ̀di*
IMPF-C^3=reach
when it reached it

b. *m-Ø-bí= 'ʔbɨ̌y*
IMPF-P^3-PNC^xc=be
it was up there

c. *m-bú= 'ncų*
IMPF-SMˆxcˆ3=fear
he was very much frightened

The sequence *gw* appears in two first-order prefixes—*gwà-* (first-person irrealis) and *gwì*$_y$- (second-person irrealis)—for which there does not seem to be a ready analysis in terms of reduction from two prefixes found in the current inventory of prefixes. While these prefixes are very likely artifacts of an earlier weakening to *w* of the sort illustrated above, they are here treated as single prefixes rather than sequences of two. Either of them may occur alone or with third-order *ší-* (eventline), but not with third-order *mí-* (imperfect), which is most likely the historical source of weakened *w*. These prefixes are illustrated in (26).

(26) a. *gwà= 'ci-he*
IRˆ1-eat-px
we might eat

b. *š-kwà= 'tų*
EL-IRˆ1=die
I might have died

c. *gwì*$_y$*= 'ʔdah-ki*
IRˆ2=give-1
you could give me (something)

d. *š-kwì*$_y$*= 'ʔño*
EL-IRˆ2=walk
you might walk

1.8. Augmentation of mutable verb roots. In addition to consonant, vowel, and tone, certain prefixes also carry one of three phonological processes that may phonologically augment a following verb root. The three processes are PALATALIZATION ($_y$), VOICING ($_v$), and NASALIZATION ($_n$). It is probable that these processes are traces of segmental differences which existed between prefixes at an earlier time but which are now reduced only to their phonological impact on a following root.[4]

[4]The stem augment was first described in Anon 1893. The appearance of the stem augment with third-person subject prefixes in certain tenses is a conspicuous feature of all Otomí languages and has been described by several linguists. The second-person-subject augmenting elements, however, are not found in all of the languages.

In respect to these processes, verb roots are either MUTABLE or IMMUTABLE. Given a root beginning with any of certain consonants, preceded by a prefix which includes one of these augmenting elements, a mutable root becomes augmented but an immutable root does not. Thus, for example, the prefix *gí-* (second-person present) includes no augmenting element, but the prefix *gì$_y$-* (centric second-person future) does. Placing these two prefixes, in (27), before the immutable stem *ʔų́ni* 'give' and the mutable stem *ʔə̀tʔe* 'do' illustrates the impact of *gì$_y$-* on the latter.[5]

(27) a. *gí= 'ʔų́ni*
P^2=give
you give it

b. *gì$_y$= 'ʔų́ni*
F^cc^2=give
you will give it

c. *gí= 'ʔə̀tʔé*
P^2=do
you do it

d. *gì$_y$= 'ʔyə́tʔe*
F^cc^2=do
you will do it

The palatal process ($_y$) manifests itself as palatalization of mutable roots beginning in *ʔ* or *h*. The voicing process ($_v$) manifests itself as (a) palatalization of mutable roots beginning in *ʔ* or *h* and as (b) voicing of mutable roots beginning with a voiceless stop or affricate. The nasal process ($_n$) manifests itself as (a) palatalization of mutable roots beginning in *ʔ* or *h*, as (b) voicing of root-initial voiceless stops and affricates, and as (c) prenasalization of mutable roots beginning with a stop or affricate.

When the context permits these phonological processes to be overtly manifested, they provide evidence for distinguishing between prefixes that are otherwise homophonous. Thus, for example in (28) and (29), prefixes

[5]To avoid providing examples at more than one level of phonological abstraction, a compromise transcription is used in which the presence of these three processes is always marked, whether or not the context is such that the following root is actually augmented or not. The effects of other phonological processes, such as the reduction of vowels and tones, or the devoicing of stops, are represented directly in the transcription as they occur after the corresponding 'rules' have applied.

distinguishing person-of-subject differ in their phonological realization only by the augment expressed on the following root. In (28a), prefixes *gá-* (simultaneous centric second-person) and *bá-* (progressive completive) occur with the unaugmented stem *tų* 'bring a heavy object', whereas the augmented form *ndų* of the same stem occurs in (28b) with the prenasalizing and voicing prefix *gà$_n$-* (simultaneous centric incompletive third-person)[6] and *bá-* (progressive completive). In (29a), prefixes *ší-* (eventline) and palatalizing *gí$_y$-* (sequential completive second-person) occur with the unaugmented stem *cəhə* 'arrive', whereas the augmented form *zəhə* of the same stem occurs in (29b) with *ší-* (eventline) and the voicing prefix *gí$_v$-* (sequential completive third-person).

(28) a. *té* *rá-'ngeʔką* *g$_y$-wá='tų* *nɨ̀r* *šəni*
what? ST-reason SQ^xc^2-PRG^C=carry cc$_2$s water^pot
Why did you bring the water pot?

b. *té* *rá-ngeʔką* *g$_n$-wá='ndų* *nɨ̀r* *šəni*
what? ST-reason SM^cc^I^3-PRG^C=carry cc$_2$s water-pot
Why had she brought the water-pot?

(29) a. *ya* *š-kí$_y$='cəh-ke*
now EL-SQ^xc^2=arrive^here-2
You had already arrived.

b. *ya* *š-kí$_v$='zəhə*
now EL-SQ^C^3=arrive^here
He had already arrived.

In regard to these three phonological processes, prefixes are of three types: (a) those which carry one of the processes and thereby cause the augmentation of a following root, (b) those which do not carry any process and therefore do not cause the augmentation of a following root, and (c) those which not only do not carry an augmenting process but which also block the application of the process by other prefixes of the first type with which it may occur. First-person prefixes, as a class, are of this third type; no matter what other prefix they occur with that would normally invoke the augmentation of a following root, that augmentation is blocked by the presence of a first-person prefix.

---

[6]The velar stop [g] of this and a few other prefixes is actually unarticulated when followed by [w], except when immediately preceded by [n] of an adjacent morpheme.

For example, the first-order prefix *rí*$_v$- (durative realis) normally invokes the augmentation of a mutable root beginning with one of following consonants: *p t c k ʔ h*. Sentence (30a) illustrates how this is so with the prefix *dà*$_v$- (centric third-person future), which does not block augmentation of the mutable root *cəhə* to *zəhə* by *rí*$_v$- (durative realis), whereas sentence (30b) illustrates how the prefix *gù*- (first-person future) does block such augmentation.

(30) a. *ngų̌ d-rí*$_v$*= 'zəhə* *ngų̌ g-rí*$_v$*= 'ʔuni*
as F^cc^3-DUR=arrive^here as F^cc^2-DUR=give
As soon as s/he arrives, give it to him/her.

b. *ngų̌ g-rí*$_v$*= 'cəhə* *ngų̌ g-rí*$_v$*= 'ʔuni*
as F^1-DUR=arrive^here as F^1-DUR=give
As soon as I arrive, I will give it to him/her.

Two other prefixes which block augmentation are the two first-order irrealis prefixes *rà*- (punctiliar irrealis) and *dì*- (durative irrealis incompletive). In (31), *gì*$_y$- (centric second-person future) would normally invoke the augmented form *hyanti* 'watch' but is blocked from doing so by *dì*- (durative irrealis incompletive).

(31) *n-g*$_y$*-rì= 'hanti-ge-hɨ*
IMPF-F^cc^2-DURir^I=watch-2-p
you (pl) might have been watching

A second- or third-person prefix may be realized solely as a stem augment. Imperative mode, for example, is unmarked as an overt prefix, but the imperative verb stem is augmented. Uninflected *ʔə̀de* 'hear' thus becomes imperative *ʔyə́de* 'listen!' In (32), the third-person prefix *bì*$_v$- occurs overtly with the verb *hẽhte*[7] 'clothe' but is reduced to the augmentation of the verb root *kɔti* 'place inside' to *gɔti*.

(32) *bì*$_v$*= 'hyéhti-hɨ rá- 'zɔ, ʔnę* $_v$*= 'gɔti-hɨ kàr hwando,*
C^3=clothe-p ST-good and C^3=place^in-p xcdfs coffin then
They dressed him nicely and placed him in the coffin then.

1.9. Interpreting homophonous prefix strings. Given the limited phonological form of verb prefixes and the radical reduction of vowels and tones when prefixes combine in a single verb, a great deal of homophony

[7]The final vowel of a verb stem ending in *e* is raised to *i* utterance medially.

results. One of the tasks of this study is, therefore, to demonstrate that such homophonous forms are in fact distinct prefixes and that they have specific differences of meaning that can be demonstrated.

The phoneme strings which ambiguously represent more than one string of prefixes are listed in (33).

(33)

í	*ì*	*á*	*à*	*ú*
dí	*dì*	*drá*	*drà*	*škrú*
ští	*ští*	*štá*	*štrà*	
gí	*gì*	*gá*	*gà*	
gwí	*grì*	*gwá*	*gwà*	
grí	*ngrì*	*ngwá*	*grà*	
škí	*škrì*	*grá*	*škà*	
škwí		*škwá*	*škrà*	
škrí		*škrá*		

The ambiguity of these strings in isolation is, of course, removed in the majority of cases by linguistic context. Some cases of ambiguity are removed, for example, where prefixes carry an augmenting element which affects a following mutable root. Not all roots are mutable, however, so that the presence of an augmenting element does not, in fact, disambiguate strings in a large number of instances.

Other elements in the larger context are more often the ones which do disambiguate such strings. Without attempting to illustrate all of the ambiguous strings in (33) or all of the possible disambiguating contexts, a few of the ambiguous strings are presented below, with a discussion of their possible interpretations in context.

Take, for example, the sequence *gwí-*, which can represent two distinct combinations of the prefix *bí-* (punctiliar excentric realis), with second-order prefixes *gí-* (second-person present) or *gí*$_v$- (sequential completive third-person), or it may represent the special case of *mí-* (imperfect) being realized as *w* and permuting with the *g* of *gí-* (second-person present) when following the negative word *hín*. Typical sentences with these three interpretations are presented in (34).

(34) a. *bì*$_v$*='ma* *gá*$_n$*='ngoH* *pɨ hár ngų pɨ habɨ*
C^3=go SM^cc^C^3=return xc at^3 house xc where?

g$_v$*-wí='ʔñęhę*
SQ^C^3-PNC^xc=come
He returned to his house from whence he had come.

b. *khà g-wí= 'ʔbɨ̀h-ke wa ya habɨ Ø-bí= 'hə kàr*
? P^2-PNC^xc=be-2 cc_1 now where? P^3-PNC^xc=stand xcs

higante
eucalyptus
Do you live just up here where the eucalyptus tree is growing?

c. *nuke hin gwí= 'ci chį*
2 NEG IMPF^P2=drink pulque
You didn't used to drink pulque.

Sentence (34a) is narrative and includes clear marking for third person in three places—as the subject of both verbs (augmentation of the second verb reducing possible ambiguity there) and as possessor of the locative noun. It follows that the third verb also has a third-person subject; any switch to second person would normally be accompanied by other evidence to that effect.

Sentences (34b) and (34c) both have such material—the suffix *-ke* (second person), in (34b), and the pronoun *nuke* (second person), in (34c), are both in apposition with the prefix *gí-* (second-person present). Both of these sentences are also taken from dialogues in which the addressee easily interprets the sentences as directly addressing him/her.

A second multiply ambiguous sequence is *grì-*, as illustrated in (35), where second-order prefixes *gí-* (second-person present), *gù-* (first-person future), and *gì$_y$-* (centric second-person future) occur with the first-order prefixes *dì-* (durative irrealis incompletive).

(35) a. *g-rì= 'hą̆-gɔ́ gwà= 'ʔdàʔ-ki*
F^1-DURir^I=have-1 IR^1=give-2
If I had it, I would give it to you.

b. *g$_y$-rì= 'hą̆-ge gwì= 'ʔdàh-ki*
F^cc^2-DURir^I=have-2 IR^2=give-1
If you had it, you would give it to me.

c. *tòhá g-rì= 'mą ya ší-Ø= 'thogi*
perhaps P^2-DURir^I=say now EL-P^3=pass
Perhaps you are saying, they have already passed by.

There is no problem of interpreting first- and second-person future prefixes in (35a) and (35b) because both verbs in each of the sentences are redundantly marked for person-of-subject by suffixes. In addition, the same person-of-subject is encoded by the prefix in the second clause. In (35c), the sentence is not easily interpreted as either having a first-person subject or as being the protasis of a contrary-to-fact condition, thus leaving the interpretation of second-person present tense and immediate irrealis which is also supported by the adverb *tòhá* 'perhaps'.

Finally, a third multiply ambiguous sequence is *škwá-*, which may represent first-, second- or third-person subjects in the prefixes *gù-* (first-person future), *gá-* (simultaneous centric second-person), and *gà$_n$-* (simultaneous centric incompletive third-person), when first-order *ší-* (eventline) and third-order *bá-* (completive progressive) occur. This is illustrated in (36).

(36) a. *ʔbɨ̀ š-k-wá='kohi, ya š-k-rú='khwah-mi*
when EL-F^1-PRG^C=come^back now EL-F^cc^2-FP=finish-d

š-k-rú='ci-wi
EL-F^cc^2-FP=eat-d
When I come back, you two will have finished eating.

b. *dú='hanti-ki ya š-k-wá='ʔę-ke nɨ, eso*
C^1=see-2 now EL-SM^cc^2-PRG^C=come-2 cc_2 that

dú='tæn-ki-tho
C^1=follow-2-AFF
I saw you when you were coming, so I just followed you here.

c. *š-∅-pá='pàtí kà š-k$_n$-wá='ʔñę̌hę*
EL-P^3-PRG^C=warm REL EL-SM^cc^C^3-PRG^C=come
He got warmed up as he came.

The sequence *škwá* in (36a) cannot be interpreted as simultaneous because of the prefix *rú-* (future perfect) in the second verb; it must be future. In (36b) it must be second-person simultaneous because of the second-person suffix *-ke* on the verb. Finally in (36c), the two verbs are in conjunct relation, so that the simultaneous third-person is expected; it is furthermore confirmed by the presence of the root augment which accompanies the third-person prefix in the mutable root *ʔę̌hę* 'come'.

While context aids the interpretation of homophonous prefix strings, it does not provide conclusive evidence in all cases, as the remainder of this study shows.

2
The Noun Phrase

This is not a full description of the Otomí noun phrase, but a brief introduction will aid the reader in interpreting the illustrations given for other purposes. The minimal form of a noun phrase is a noun with preposed determiner. Its prototypical function is to occupy a nominal constituent of a clause. It may be expanded to include additional elements such as a quantifier, a preposed descriptive modifier, or a postposed modifier—all of which may occur in combination with each other.

These elements occur in fairly rigid order when occurring together, namely, quantifier, determiner, preposed modifier, noun, and postposed modifier. Determiners are discussed first (§§2.1–5), as the most common elements to occur with nouns, followed by brief remarks about quantifiers (§2.6), preposed descriptive modifiers (§2.7), and postposed modifiers (§2.8).

A final section in this chapter (§2.9), briefly presents how verb prefixes may be associated with nonactive predicates based on stative verbs or nouns.

2.1–5 Determiners

A fairly large number of determiners occurs with nouns in the noun phrase. These are presented below in five sets—indefinite, $centric_1$ (definite), $centric_2$ (definite), excentric (definite), and locative, respectively. Each of these sets includes two nonpossessive forms as well as several possessive forms.

(37) a. *ɨ̀r* (ins, indefinite singular)
∅ (inp, indefinite plural)
(g)ɨ̀m (in1, indefinite first-person possessive)
èr, rì (in2, indefinite second-person possessive)
ɨ́r (ins3, indefinite singular third-person possessive)
í (inp3, indefinite plural third-person possessive)

b. *ną̀r* (cc_1s, centric$_1$ singular)
yà (cc_1p, centric$_1$ plural)[8]
ną̀m (cc_1s1, centric$_1$ singular first-person possessive)
yą̀m (cc_1p1, centric$_1$ plural first-person possessive)
ną́r (cc_1s3, centric$_1$ singular third-person possessive)

c. *nɨ̀r* (cc_2s, centric$_2$ singular)
yɨ̀ (cc_2p, centric$_2$ plural)
nɨ̀m (cc_2s1, centric$_2$ singular first-person possessive)
yɨ̀m (cc_2p1, centric$_2$ plural first-person possessive)
nìr (ccs2, centric singular second-person possessive)
yìr (ccp2, centric plural second-person possessive)
nɨ́r (cc_2s3, centric$_2$ singular third-person possessive)
yí (ccp3, centric plural third-person possessive)

d. *kàr* (xcs, excentric singular)
kɨ̀ (xcp, excentric plural)
kàm (xcs1, excentric singular first-person possessive)
kɨ̀m (xcp1, excentric plural first-person possessive)
kèr (xcs2, excentric singular second-person possessive)
kìr (xcp2, excentric plural second-person possessive)
kár (xcs3, excentric singular third-person possessive)
kí (xcp3, excentric plural third-person possessive)

e. *hâr* (at^s, locative singular)[9]
há (at^p, locative plural)
hám (at^1, locative first-person possessive)
hèr (at^2, locative second-person possessive)
hár (at^3, locative third-person possessive)

---

[8]This form occurs in my data as both *yà* and *yą̀*. Its occurrence is not frequent, with the result that I cannot be sure if one or the other was transcribed incorrectly.

[9]This word *hâr* is the only word in the language known to occur with a phonologically contrastive tone downglide, here indicated by circumflex (ˆ) over the vowel. This downglide results from the merging of *há* 'at' and *ɨ̀r* 'be'.

2.1. Indefinite determiners. The first set of indefinite determiners listed in (37a) has eight distinct forms, but three of them are phonological variants of one another. The first two unpossessed forms are morphologically the most simple. Possessed forms may be considered inflected forms of these, but the complexity of the phonological result of this inflection makes it unproductive to treat them as other than grammatical units. This first set of indefinite determiners are illustrated in (38). In a sentence following *hín* (negative), such as (38d), they occur with an initial *g* and high tone.[10] The second-person form *rì* occurs with nouns that name objects closely associated with the possessor, such as 'heart' and 'house'; *èr* occurs with nouns that name less closely related objects. Notice in (38h) that number distinctions in the determiner denote the number of referents of the associated noun rather than the number of possessors.

(38) a. *ya šì ɨr ánima ʔbɨ́*
now EL ins soul now
Now it is a soul.

b. *sá hín gy-rá='pàʔti ∅ hmę, gìy='cǐ*
why? NEG F^cc^2-PNC^cc=heat inp tortilla F^cc^2=eat now then
Why don't you heat some tortillas and eat them?

c. *ɨ́r tʔį̀šų́ kàm tʔį̀šų́ ɨ̀m cí ʔbǽhtó*
ins3 daughter xcs1 daughter in1 little grandchild
My daughter's daughter is my little grandchild.

d. *hín gɨ́m mæhti gɔ pa gù='ʔdah-ki-wi*
NEG in1 possession-1 that F^1=give-2-d
It is not mine to give to you two.

e. *khà èr mæhtl-ge yɨ̀ zųʔwę*
? in2 possession-2 cc_2p animal
Are these animals (possessions of) yours?

f. *hín ge š-ky-rì='kąhki rì ʔyæ*
NEG be EL-F^cc^2-DURir=cut^off in2 hand
Don't be cutting off your hand.

---

[10]The negative word has a full form *hį́ną* and two shorter forms, *hį́* and *hín*. The second of these shorter forms occurs preceding stops other than *ʔ*, the first shorter one does not.

g. *š-tà=t-'ʔɔh-pi* *ɨ́r* *hñąkhą*
EL-F^cc^3=PASS-request-BEN ins3 prayer^for^dead
They will request a prayer for his/her soul.

h. *pe* *goo* *í* *bąhci* *dú='ʔəm-bi*
but four inp3 child C^1=bear-BEN
But I bore him four children.

The remaining nonlocative determiners—centric$_1$, centric$_2$, and excentric—are definite and it may be argued that they consist of an initial deictic element which is followed by one of the indefinite forms. Once again, however, the phonological fusion which occurs in these situations has led me to present them here as single, albeit complex, units. The deictic elements in these determiners are based on the forms listed in (39).

(39) *ną́* (cc$_1$s, centric$_1$ singular)
yá (cc$_1$p, centric$_1$ plural)
nɨ́ (cc$_2$s, centric$_2$ singular)
yɨ́ (cc$_2$p, centric$_2$ plural)
ką́ (xcs, excentric singular)
kɨ́ (xcp, excentric plural)

The six deictic elements in (39) are anaphoric pronouns which occur following and in apposition to noun phrases, within a clause. Thus, for example, in (40), an anaphoric pronoun follows a noun phrase in concordance with its determiner to anaphorically emphasize the identity of the referent of the noun phrase. The pronoun may follow the noun phrase directly (40a) or it may occur separated from it at the end of the clause (40b).

(40) a. *tó* *yí* *mǽhti* *yɨ̀* *wàdé* *yɨ́*
who? ccp3 possession cc$_2$p chicken cc$_2$p
To whom do those chickens belong?

b. *yɨ̀* *zǎ* *yí* *mǣ̌hti* *kàr* *rita* *yɨ́*
cc$_2$p wood ccp3 possession xcs Rita cc$_2$p
That firewood belongs to Rita.

2.2. Centric$_1$ determiners. The five centric$_1$ determiners listed in (37b) are definite and locate the referent of an associated noun right at the deictic center. This set is defective in not having distinct forms for second-person possessor or for plural third-person possessor. The probable reason for this is discussed in the next section. These forms are also less common than other determiners, apparently for pragmatic reasons; they are needed less often in the communication situation than other determiners. I do not, as a matter of fact, have even one example of the plural first-person form in my written corpus, even though I propose here that it is a valid form. The use of the remaining four of these determiners is illustrated in (41).

(41) a. *nậr ngṳ̀ nậ́*
cc₁s house cc₁s
this house here

b. *hín gí='nèstá-wi yà š-kúy='kậ́ší wa, yà media*
NEG P^2=need-d cc₁p EL-C^2=hang cc₁ cc₁p stocking
You do not need these things that are hanging here, these stockings.

c. *gè nậ̀m ʔyæ-gɔ nậ́*
be cc₁s1 hand-1 cc₁s
This is my hand!

d. *gè nậ́r sweter kàm ʔñowi*
be cc₁s3 sweater xcs1 friend
This is my friend's sweater.

2.3. Centric$_2$ determiners. The eight determiners listed in (37c) are definite and locate the referent within sight of the deictic center. Five of them contrast with the centric$_1$ determiners by denoting referents somewhat removed from the immediate deictic center but still relatively near at hand or in-sight; whereas three of them are ambiguously centric in that they range over both the near centric$_1$ location as well as more distant centric$_2$ locations.

The five centric$_2$ determiners and the three ambiguously centric ones are illustrated in (42). The examples in (42c) and (42g) illustrate how a plural suffix on a noun specifies number for the possessor indicated by the determiner rather than for the referent of the noun itself.

(42) a. *š-tá='mă-gɔ má co-gɔ nɨ̀r hæʔmi*
EL-SM^1=go-1 go leave-1 cc₂s document
I am going to go and leave this document (there).

b. *ʔì= 'ʔbɨ̀H yɨ̀ dohto ʔì= 'hą ɨ̀r reloh*
P^3=be cc$_2$p doctor P^3=have ins clock
There are doctors (here) who have a watch.

c. *m-bú= 'ncų ya nɨ̀m phani-he*
IMPF-SM^xc^3=fear now cc$_2$s1 horse-1x
Our horse was very much frightened then.

d. *ʔnà ʔnà ʔnà ngwàdí ∅-rí$_V$= 'mɔ̀H yɨ̀m ʔyó*
one one one side P^3-DUR=stand cc$_2$p1 dog
My dogs are standing one on each side of me.

e. *té rá$_n$-ngeʔką g$_y$-wá= 'tų nìr šəni*
what? ST-reason SQ^xc^2-PRG^C=carry ccs2 water-pot
Why did you bring your water-pot?

f. *tengų š-kú= 'khųti yìr khoʔmi-zæšthi gí= 'tįʔti*
how^much? EL-C^2=pay ccp2 cover-sandal P^2=wear
How much did you pay for the shoes you are wearing?

g. *nin te cɨ̀ ∅-dì= 'ʔbɨ̀h-ti-hɨ nɨ́r ngų-hɨ*
EMPH what? few P^3-DURir=be-AFF-p cc$_2$s3 house-p
They are hardly ever at home (i.e. their house).

h. *yɨ̀ zǎ yí mæhti kàr rita yɨ́*
cc$_2$p wood ccp3 possession xcs Rita cc$_2$p
These sticks (of firewood) over here, they belong to Rita.

2.4. Excentric determiners. Where centric determiners begin with *n* or *y*, excentric determiners begin with *k*, as indicated in (37d). Like the centric determiners, they are definite in reference, thereby contrasting with the indefinite series. They are illustrated in (43).

(43) a. *té rá$_n$-ngeʔką g$_n$-wá= 'ndų kàr šəni*
what? ST-reason SM^cc^C^3-PRG^C=carry xcs water-pot
Why had she brought the water-pot?

b. *gege ∅-bà=ndò- 'tæn kɨ̀ khąʔnį rá$_n$- 'ngų*
ANA P^3-PRG^I=greatly-follow xcp person ST-many
A lot of people are coming, (they are) very much following him.

c. *n-d-rá= 'ʔbɨh-ʔbe pɨ ʔmundɔ kàm khwą̀dą*
IMPF-P1-PNC^cc=be-dx xc Mexico xcs1 brother^of^male
I was in Mexico City with my brother.

d. *š-tá= 'tųʔti-he kɨ̀m wade-he*
EL-SM^1=tie^feet-px xcp1 chicken-px
We had tied the legs of our chickens.

e. *ngų̌ šì gàn= 'mąn kàm ʔñowi, Ø-rán-ndò= 'nthį*
as EL SM^cc^I^3=say xcs1 companion P^3-ST-greatly-difficult

kèr hñą-hɨ
xcs2 language-p
As my companion says, your (pl) language is very difficult.

f. *gì= 'mphɔdi, š-tá= 'tɔm-bi-ki kìr dą́htų*
F^cc^2=shepherd EL-SM^1=buy-BEN-2 xcp2 clothing
Take care of my animals and I will buy clothes for you.

g. *bú=ʔnà- 'kʔą ya kár macho kí sario*
SM^xc^3=sudden-appear now xcs3 mule xcp3 Cesario
Then from over there suddenly the mule of Cesario's family appeared (from behind something).

2.5. Locative determiners. In addition to the three sets of determiners which occur with nouns in nominal positions of clauses, there is a smaller subset of determiners which mark a noun phrase as locative with non-motion verbs or allative with motion verbs. Items referenced by such locative noun phrases are, by definition, excentric in relation to the deictic center. These determiners, based on *há* (at) as first element, are listed in (37e) and illustrated in (44).

(44) a. *ʔǎ dí= 'mæ-wi nɨ̀ hâr do*
now SQ^cc₂^2=go^d-d cc₂ at^s stone
You two go over there where the stone is now.

b. *ya kà n-dí= 'pæʔci-hɨ, š-tú= 'gasto-hɨ há Ø médiko*
now REL IMPF-P^1=have-p EL-C^1=spend-p at^p inp doctor
Now, that which used to have we have spent on doctors.

c. *hín gì=t-'hægi wà hám luga-he*
NEG P^3=PASS-allow cc_1 at^1 place-1px
That isn't allowed here at our (excl) place.

d. *gú='ma gí$_y$='koH pɨ̀ hèr ngų pɨ̀ habɨ gí*
C2=go SQ^xc^2=return xc at^2 house xc where SQ^xc^2=come
You went, returning to your house, whence you had come.

e. *dú='šiH kàr nąnạ da$_v$='má d-rí$_v$='ʔun kàr*
C^1=tell xcs older^woman F^cc^3=go SQ^I^3-DUR=give xcs

ʔñįthį pɨ̀ hár ngų
medicine xc at^3 house
I told the woman to go and give him/her the medicine there at her house.

2.6. Quantifiers. Once again, no attempt is made here to describe the variety of quantifiers that may occur in Otomí. Simply note that a quantifier may initiate a noun phrase.

(45) a. *yòhto kheyæ*
seven year
seven years

b. *ʔnà thɔy*
one debt
a debt

(46) a. *goo í bąhci*
four inp3 child
his four children

b. *ntero kɨ̀ mbəhə*
all xcp ladino
all of the Spanish-speakers

The numeral 'one' may also be inflected by some of the same endings found in determiners to specify definiteness or person-of-possessor, as indicated in (47) and illustrated in (48).

(47) *ʔnàr* 'one (indefinite)'
ʔnàm 'one (first-person possession)'

(48) a. *ʔnàr ci tɨhki ɨ̀r tʔæy*
one^in little small ins wheat
some little bit of wheat

b. *gù= 'cæhti ʔnàm hmę*
F^1=have^alone one^1 corncake
I'm going to eat just a tortilla (of mine).

2.7. Preposed descriptive modifiers. A preposed modifier may intervene between a numeral (48a) or determiner (49) and a following noun. In this context, the modifier is usually an uninflected adjective, although a simple relative clause may occasionally also be found in preposed position (49c), as may a very small set of nouns (49d).

(49) a. *nɨ̀r mægi ʔñəhə nɨ́*
cc_2s darn! man cc_2s
this darn man

b. *kár cí bą̀hci*
xcs3 little child
his/her little child

c. *nɨ̀r cí n-kʔóʔti nkhə́dé bą̀hcí*
cc_2s small REFL-take^off skirt child
this little child who takes off her skirt

d. *ʔnàr bą̀hcí míši*
one^in child cat
a young cat

2.8. Postposed modifiers. A verb may also follow a noun as modifier, and in this context may be either a stative verb occurring with the stative prefix *rá$_n$-*, as in (50), or an active verb, as in (51).

(50) a. *kɨ̀ thą rá$_n$- 'noho*
xcp maize^ear ST-large
the large ears of corn

b. *nɨ̀r dą́htų rá$_n$- 'ntʔăši*
cc_2s clothing ST-white
the white clothing

(51) a. *kàr ʔbəhñą ką́, d-rá='ʔęh-me ką́*
xcs vow xcs P^1-PNC^cc=come-px xcs
that vow we are coming (to pay)

b. *yìr khoʔmi-zæšthi gí='tįʔti*
ccp2 cover-sandal P2=wear
the shoes you are wearing

Since such postposed modifiers are always verbs, whether derived or not, it can be argued that they are, in fact, minimal relative clauses;[11] but there is also a relative word *kà*, undoubtedly the basis for forming the excentric determiners of §2.3, which may be present to clearly mark a relative clause in this postposed position, as in (52).

(52) a. *kàr ndò dąhcə kà Ø-ríᵥ='nįgi nɨ́*
xcs big planet REL P^3-DUR=appear cc_2
the big star that appears over there

b. *kàr za kà Ø-rà='mphɨni*
xcs wood REL P^3-PNC^ir=smoke
the piece of wood that's smoking (down in the fire)

c. *kàr carro kà gáₙ='mɔh-mɨ*
xcs bus REL SM^cc^C^3=go^p-p
the bus that they went on

If we recognize the relative word as a type of determiner, it is moot as to whether the postposed 'determined' noun should be considered syntactically subordinate to the preceding determined noun or whether it is simply appositive with it. Any of the other determiners may also occur in this position.

(53) *kɨ̀ ndò khąʔñį kɨ̀ bìᵥ='gąti*
xcp big person xcp C^3=descend^into
the adults who went down into (the water)

---

[11]This cannot be pursued here; but if such verbal adjectives are to be treated as minimal relative clauses, they should presumably also be considered to occur with the zero form of the third-person present-tense prefix. Thus, *Ø=ráₙ-'noho* '(which) is large' and *Ø=ráₙ-'ntʔăši* '(which) is white'.

Such 'determined' clauses can, in fact, stand alone as noun phrases, without a noun preceding them, further attesting to their syntactic independence, giving weight to the appositive interpretation.

(54) *kɨ̀ mí-∅='he kɨ̀ dąhtų rá$_n$-'ntʔaši*
xcp IMPF-P^3=wear xcp clothing ST-white
those who were wearing the white clothing.

In a sequence of two determined noun phrases, the determiner of the first is possessive, and the second noun phrase is in cross-reference with the person-of-possessor of the first determiner.

(55) a. *hár ngų kèr me*
at^3 house xcs2 mother
at your mother's house

b. *kár ʔbæhñą kàr masedonio*
xcs3 woman xcs Macedonio
the wife of Macedonio

c. *kár macho kí sario*
xcs3 mule xcp3 Cesario
the mule of Cesario's family

d. *kí karta kàm me*
xcp3 letter xcs1 mother
my mother's letters

e. *í bą̀hci kàr abraham*
inp3 child xcs Abraham
the children of Abraham

2.9. Nonactive Predicates. There are two forms which permit stative verbs or nouns, respectively, to be associated with second- and third-order verb prefixes. The first of these is the stative prefix *rá$_n$-*, which derives a stative verb from an adjective or active verb root; the second is the copular verb root *ɨ̀r-* 'be'.

The place of adjectives in the noun phrase was introduced immediately above, where it was shown that a simple adjective may precede and modify a noun, but occurs only as a stative verb in postposed position. This is illustrated once again in (56).

(56) a. *nɨ̀r kʔăšti dɔ̀ni*
cc₂s yellow flower
this yellow flower

b. *nɨ̀r dɔ̀ni $rá_n$- 'nkʔăšti*
cc₂s flower ST-yellow
this yellow flower (*lit.* that is yellow)

An adjective may also function outside of a noun phrase, as the predicator of a clause, in which case it must normally occur as a derived stative verb, with *$rá_n$-* (verbalizer).

(57) *m-Ø=$rá_n$-cí-'zɔ n-gá$_n$='šɔdi*
IMPF-P^3=ST-great-good IMPF-SM^cc^C^3=sing
S/he used to sing beautifully.

In this context, *$rá_n$-* permits both second- and third-order verb prefixes to occur with the adjective root. Since first-order prefixes may not occur with *$rá_n$-*, it is moot as to whether it should itself be considered a first-order inflectional affix like those described in §6, or whether—as a verb-forming prefix—it should be considered a stem formative and, therefore, as part of derived verbal stems. To distinguish it from those that are clearly inflectional, it is here placed to the right of the equals sign (=).

The simplest cases of stative verbs as predicates are found in third-person present-tense clauses where the derived verb is considered to occur with the zero form of the third-person present-tense prefix, but other prefixes may occur as well.

(58) a. *Ø=$rá_n$-'nte*
P^3-ST=tall
S/he is tall, *or* It is high.

b. *Ø=$rá_n$-'ncæ*
P^3=ST-cold
It is cold.

c. *Ø=$rá_n$-'ngų*
P^3=ST-many
It is a lot, *or* There are many.

d. *∅=rán-ndò-'zoʔmi-te yɨ̀ khąʔnį*
P^3=ST-greatly-critical cc2p person
These people are very critical.

e. *dv=rán-'zɔ́ kàr chį̌*
F^cc^3=ST-good xcs pulque
The pulque will be good.

With numerals and the relative word, *rán-* is used to express ordinal numbers.

(59) a. *kà ∅=rán-'hñųh-pa*
REL P^3=ST-three-day
the third day

b. *kà ∅=rán-'kɨtʔa kheyæ*
REL P^3=ST-five year
the fifth year

The stative prefix *rán-* is not fully realized in negative statements. Only its augment is present. In this context, a derived stem may occur directly as predicator with second- and third-order verb prefixes.

(60) a. *hín gì=n-'nte*
NEG P^3=ST-tall
S/he isn't tall, *or* It isn't high.

b. *hį́ mí-∅=n-'ncæ*
NEG IMPF-P^3=ST-cold
It wasn't cold.

It is common for a clause based on a stative verb to have an impersonal third-person subject. For a quality or state to be predicated of a first- or second-person, the latter is encoded as syntactic object, as in (61a) and (61b). Tense-aspect other than simple present-tense is expressed with *rán-* by use of the third-order prefix *mí-* (imperfect) or the second-order prefix *dàv-* (centric third-person future).

(61) a. *m-∅=rán-ndò-'ncæ-gi*
IMPF-P^3=ST-greatly-cold-1
I was very cold (*lit.* it was very cold to me).

b. *m-Ø=rán-'nzæʔ-ki*
IMPF-P^3=ST-strong-2
You were strong (*lit.* there was strength to you).

c. *m-Ø=rán-'nkhų kì dæ̀thą́*
IMPF-P^3=ST-bitter xcp corn
That corn was bitter.

(62) a. *dᵥ=rán-'zɔ kì chį šųdi*
F^cc^3=ST-good xcp maguey^wine tomorrow
That maguey wine will be good tomorrow.

b. *kà pé š-tᵥ=rán-'yo š-tàᵥ='ñɨti ya*
REL again EL-F^cc^3=ST-two EL-F^cc^3=go^in now
the one who will go in next

A clause with a stative verb is marked as belonging to the eventline or as the principal statement in the same way as other clauses, by use of the third-order prefix *ší-* (timeline) and the time encoded is concordant with that of a coreferential clause in the same context.

(63) *ya š-Ø=ná-ndò-'ngų Ø=rán-'ʔɨ́*
now EL-P^3=ST-great-many P^3=PNC^cc-painful
Now it hurts an awful lot.

While the use of an object suffix to reference the person qualified by a stative verb is normal, as in (61a) and (61b), it is also possible for nonthird persons to be referenced by second-order prefixes with such verbs, as in (64), where morphological parallelism is maintained with an associated clause.

(64) *ʔbɨ̀ n-d='ɨr bą̀hci-gɔ, n-d=rán-'cʔoʔyo*
when IMPF-P^1=be child-1 IMPF-P^1=ST-greedy
When I was a child, I was greedy.

The copular verb *ɨ̀r* 'be' permits a noun to be associated with second- and third-order verb prefixes in the form of a nominal complement. Clauses based on this structure predicate singular identificational referents. The zero form of the second-order third-person present-tense prefix is normally used in this context, but a reduced form of *gì-* (third-person present) occurs with *hín* (negative). As in the case of stative verbs, nominal complements normally encode nonthird-persons by the use of object suffixes.

(65) a. *d= 'ɨ́r mæ̀gi bą̀hci-gɔ, ʔną́*
P^1=be darn child-1 say
I am a stubborn child, s/he says.

b. *nùke g= 'ɨ́r ʔñəhə*
2 P^2=be man
You are a man.

c. *Ø= 'ɨ̀r hyɔhte nɨ̀r khąʔnį*
P^3=be deceiver cc₂s person
This person is a deceiver.

d. *hín g=ɨ́r nxųhñą ką́*
NEG P^3=be bother xcs
That is no bother.

When the identity of a dual or plural nominal referent is predicated, the copular verb *ɨ̀r* is not used. In this context, second-order verb prefixes may occur directly preposed to the noun root along with one of four person-number suffixes which distinguish dual, plural, inclusive, and exclusive person.

(66) a. *dí= 'ʔbæhñą-ʔbe*
P^1=woman-dx
We two (excl) are women.

b. *gí= 'mæ̨thri-tho-hɨ*
P^2=liar-AFF-p
You (pl) are indeed liars.

c. *kàr david kor lasaro Ø= 'ci ʔñəhə-wi*
xcs David and^ins Lazarus P^3=small man-d
David and Lazarus are (two) little boys.

In (67a), the impersonal noun *trábaho* 'hard work' (Sp. *trabajo*) is the predicate, with the following noun phrase as its subject. The fronting of the predicate probably indicates emphasis. With negative *hín* in (67b), the *gí-* form of the third-person present-tense prefix is required with the nominal predicate, as with verbal predicates.

(67) a. *∅='trábaho ya ɨ̀m ʔbæfi-gɔ-he*
P^3=hard^work now in1 work-1-px
Our work is really hard work.

b. *hín gí='khąʔnį yɨ́*
NEG P^3=person cc₂p
These are not people.

Social relationships are expressed by a subset of nouns, including kinship terms, which normally occur with possessed determiners in the noun phrase. When such nouns occur as predicates with nonthird-person subjects, person-of-subject is marked obliquely by an object suffix. Third-person subjects, on the other hand, when expressed, are referenced by a pronoun or noun phrase.

(68) a. *ɨ̀m nkhų-ki*
in1 sister-2
You are my sister (man speaking).

b. *èr nkhų-ge ką́*
in2 sister-2 xcs
That one is your sister (male addressee).

c. *hį́ ɨ́r hmų̌-ki*
NEG ins3 owner-2
You aren't its (the dog's) owner.

d. *nùgɔ-he í bą̀hci-gi-he kàr abraham*
1-px inp3 child-1-px xcs Abraham
We (excl) are Abraham's children.

e. *ɨ́r bą̀hci kàm khùhwǽ nɨ́*
ins3 child xcs1 sister cc₂s
This one is my sister's child (woman speaking).

f. *pe kàr ʔñɔ́hə, gégé mí-∅='mą̀di, komo ɨ́r thæšyakhą̂*
but xcs man ANA IMPF-P^3=love because ins3 godchild
But that man, he loved him, because he is his godchild.

To express future or irrealis when predicating the identity of a nominal referent, second-order prefixes occur with the copular verb with the nominal as complement.

(69) a. *ʔbɨ̀ g= 'ɨ̀r bą̀hci-gɔ, gwà= 'ʔɔ̀h-pi kàm ta ɨ̀m me*
when IR^1=be child-1 IR^1=request-BEN xcs1 father in1 mother
If I were a child, I would ask my father and my mother.

b. *ʔbɨ̀ g= 'ɨ̀r mįngų wa, gwì$_y$= 'pą̌di*
when IR^2=be native cc_1 IR^2=know
If you were a native here, you would know how (to do it.)

c. *khà d= 'ɨ̀r ʔbǣhñą̀, wǎ d= 'ɨ̀r ʔñə̀hə*
? F^xc^3=be woman or F^xc^3=be man
Will it be a girl or a boy?

d. *šǐ kàr zǎ kà ∅-rá= 'ʔbɔH pɨ̀, khà ∅-d$_V$= '*
re xcs wood REL P^3=PNC^cc-stand xc ? P^3-DURir^C=be

ánima ya ką́, siendo ɨ̀r zǎ
soul now xcs be ins wood
As for that piece of wood standing over there, would that be a soul, since it is wood?

When such a nominal referent is possessed, on the other hand, future or irrealis prefixes are joined to the possessive determiner rather than the copular verb.

(70) a. *nùʔbɨ ∅-d$_V$= 'ɨ̀m bą̀hci-gɔ nɨ́, gwà= 'ciš hâr doctor*
if P^3-DURir^C=in1 child-1 cc_2s IR^1=take at^s doctor
If this were my child, I would take him/her to the doctor.

b. *ʔbɨ̀ ∅-d$_V$= 'ɨ̀r mǣhti-sæ nɨ̀r ngų . . .*
when P^3-DURir^C=ins possess-own cc_2s house
If this house belonged to you personally . . .

c. *to ∅-d$_V$= 'ɨ́r ʔbǣhñą̀ ʔbɨ́*
in P^3-DURir^C=ins woman when
Whose wife would she be then?

There is much more to be said about Otomí nominals, but this introduction to the noun phrase and related material will perhaps aid the reader in interpreting the noun phrase portions of illustrations used throughout the study, which now proceeds directly to its main focus, verb prefixes.

3
Primary Second-order Prefixes

Second-order prefixes have the heaviest functional load of verb prefixes. It is normal for every Otomí verb to have a second-order prefix and second-order prefixes are the only ones which may normally occur as the sole prefix of an Otomí verb. There are two sets of second-order prefixes—PRIMARY prefixes which ground a clause in time and space and CONJUNCT prefixes which do not. By "grounding in time and space," I mean (following Payne 1989) that primary prefixes encode the four deictic operations which characterize independent clauses. They are the spatial location (sometimes direction) of situation or event, the time of the event, participant reference, and realis mode. These are all marked by primary second-order prefixes. Conjunct prefixes either refer to a different time or place from that of the deictic center (referenced by grounded clauses in the immediate context) or they fail to identify person-of-subject, in either case failing thereby to fully ground a clause; they will be dealt with in the next chapter. Primary prefixes are discussed in this chapter.

Primary second-order prefixes encode three distinct persons-of-subject, three categories of time reference, and two categories of location or direction in respect to the deictic center. They all encode realis mode—events or situations reported as factual.

Taking tense-aspect as the primary organizing principle, the set of primary second-order prefixes are presented in (71) as forming three subsets which denote present tense, completive aspect, and future tense, respectively. Three categories of person-of-subject—first, second, third—are then found to be distinguished in all three subsets. Finally, centric and excentric location in reference to the deictic center are distinguished for nonfirst persons in the future-tense set.

(71) a. *dí-* (P^1, first-person present)
gí- (P^2, second-person present)
gì-, *ʔì-*, *∅* (P^3, third-person present)

b. *dú-* (C^1, first-person completive)
gú$_y$- (C^2, second-person completive)
bì$_v$- (C^3, third-person completive)

c. *gù-* (F^1, first-person future)
gì$_y$- (F^cc^2, centric second-person future)
dà$_v$- (F^cc^3, centric third-person future)
gù- (F^xc^2, excentric second-person future)
dù- (F^xc^3, excentric third-person future)

Each of these three subsets is discussed and illustrated in the next three sections.

3.1. Present-tense prefixes. The first subset of five primary second-order prefixes (including zero) encode person-of-subject and present tense. As is the case in many languages, Otomí present-tense prefixes are not, strictly speaking, TENSE prefixes; they are atemporal. They do not index time as such. The label PRESENT is used for convenience. The semantic force of these prefixes actually ranges across the aspectual categories HABITUAL, CONTINUOUS, PROGRESSIVE, and ITERATIVE, depending upon the choice of verb and on its context. The examples which follow of the several present-tense prefixes document this full range of meanings.

These prefixes are illustrated in (72) as they occur when no other verb prefix is present. The distribution of the three variants of the third-person present tense is predictable in terms of the presence of particular morphemes in the context. The form *gì-* (72c) occurs with *hin* (negative) or with *ší-* (eventline) when no first-order prefix is present; the form *ʔì-* (72d) occurs when it is the only prefix on the verb, in formal speech; and the zero form (72e) occurs in all other prefix combinations as well as in informal conversational speech when no other prefixes are present and the subject has been previously identified in the context.

(72) a. *hín te dí='ʔñi̧h-kɔ miši*
NEG in P^1=have-1 cat
I don't own any cat.

b. *dí= 'ʔóki-bi nɨ́r ñą́ nɨ̀r cʔɨ̀tó*
P^1=cut^off-BEN cc₂s3 top cc₂s branch^tip
I am cutting off the tip end of this branch.

c. *kha gí= 'hanti nɨ̀r ngų nɨ ∅-rá= 'khǎ nɨ*
? P^2=see cc₂s house cc₂ P^3-PNCcc-located cc₂
Do you see that house over there?

d. *hín gì=t- 'hægi wa ham luga-he*
NEG P^3=PASS-allow cc₁ at^1 place-1px
That isn't allowed here at our (excl) place.

e. *ya š-kì= 'ʔǎn-tho gàₙ= 'ʔñó*
now EL-P^3=stoop-AFF SM^cc^P^3=walk
Now s/he stoops over when s/he walks.

f. *ʔì= 'ʔbɨ̀h-ti kàm ta*
P^3=be-AFF xcs1 father
My father is still living.

g. *∅= 'khà ∅ ncʔɔya ɨr šųdi*
P^3=make inp rest ins tomorrow
Tomorrow is a day of rest.

3.2. Completive-aspect prefixes. The second subset of primary second-order prefixes, listed in (71b), encode person-of-subject and completive aspect, where completive aspect views a situation perfectively, in the sense of Comrie, "as a single whole, without distinction of the various separate phases that make up that situation" (1976:16). These forms thus usually encode situations which have occurred in the past.

In (73), each of the three completive forms is illustrated as it occurs with no other verb prefix present within the verb.

(73) a. *nugɔ, komo n-d= 'ɨr bą̀hci-gɔ, dú= 'tæn-di kɨ̀ nd*
1 because IMPF-P^1=be child-1 C^1=follow-AFF xcp big

khąʔñį kɨ̀ bìᵥ= 'gąti
person xcp C^3=descend^into
I, being a child, just followed the adults who went down into (the water).

b. *yǎnɨ n-dá='ʔe̜he̜, pero gú='meya-gi*
far IMPF-SM^1=come but C^2=know-1
I was coming a long way off, but you recognized me.

c. *bì~v~='hye kí da̜htu̜, ʔbɨ́*
C^3=dress xcp3 clothing then
He put on his clothes then.

Although completive aspect prefixes usually occur in past-time contexts, they are sometimes used in the protasis of a condition to encode a point in future time perceived as previous to that of the apodasis. They may occur in both positive and negative statements, but conjunct forms are more likely to occur in negative statements.

(74) a. *ʔbɨ̀ ʔbæto dú='tù-gɔ, khà gì~y~='nzoni*
then first C^1=die-1 ? F^cc^2=weep
If I die first, will you cry?

b. *ʔbɨ̀ hín dú='ma-gɔ, gì~y~='šiH kèr khùhwǽ d*
then NEG C^1=go-1 F^cc^2=tell xcs2 sister^of^woman F^cc^3=go
If I don't go, tell your sister to go.

c. *ʔbɨ̀ bì~v~='zə-hə, š-tà~v~='dɨ̀h-ki-wi*
then C^3=arrive-cc$_1$ EL-F^cc^3=burn-1-di
If they arrive here, they will burn you and me.

3.3. Future-tense prefixes. The third subset of five primary second-order prefixes, listed in (71c), encode person-of-subject, future tense—where future tense views a situation as anticipated or intended at the deictic center—and relative distance from the deictic center. Each of the three centric future forms is illustrated in (75), occurring with no other verb prefix present within the verb. These centric forms are chosen when the future action or situation will occur at or near the deictic center of the immediate context. Notice in (75b) that the second-person verb of arrival denotes motion culminating at the deictic center.

(75) a. *gù='cæhti ʔnàm hme̜*
F^1=have^alone one^1 corncake
I'm going to eat my tortilla, just by itself.

b. *kháʔmɨ gì$_{y}$= 'cəH ya*
when? F^cc^2=arrive-cc$_1$ now
When will you arrive here then?

c. *gù= 'ʔmìʔ-ʔbe, dà$_{V}$= 'ʔwį̣n-gi, dà$_{V}$= 'mantene-gi*
F^1=live-dx F^cc^3=feed-1 F^cc^3=support-1
I will live with him; he will feed me and support me.

d. *nìr cí ʔyo, dà$_{V}$= 'zà kàm ʔyo-gɔ-he*
ccs2 little dog F^cc^3=bite xcs1 dog-1-px
Your pet dog! Our (excl) dog will bite him!

In narrative, it is not rare to find the future tense encoding a time in the past subsequent to that encoded in a previous clause where the tense is completive or imperfect, as in (76).

(76) *nuya kɨ́, sɨ š-tà$_{V}$= 'nde ya, ora dà$_{V}$= 'hyɨši*
now xcp well EL-F^cc^3=get^late now time F^cc^3=whistle now

ʔeš gù= 'tæni, má, masque hį́ ʔbé n-dá= 'ci,
immediately F^1=follow go although NEG yet IMPF-SM^1=eat

n-dí= 'pa
IMPF-P^1=go
Those ones, well, when it was evening, at the time when they would whistle, right away I would follow them, (I would) go even though I had not yet eaten, I used to go.

A true imperative verb simply lacks a person-of-subject prefix, as in the first clause of (77a), but the second-person future prefix may also be used as a mild command, as in the remaining clauses of (77).

(77) a. *cɨhti ya; gì$_{y}$= 'ʔun-gi kár ʔba*
nurse! now F^cc^2=give-AFF xcs3 milk
Now nurse him! Give him (his) milk.

b. *gì$_{y}$= 'ʔñį́š yɨ̀ dạhtų hâr nthạhį*
F^cc^2=hang cc$_2$p clothing at^s rope
Hang up the clothes on the clothesline.

c. *hín gìy= 'ma gìy= 'hñą̣ʔmi kí*
NEG F^cc^2=go F^cc^2=take^out xcp
Now don't you start taking those things out.[12]

The third-person future prefix of this subset may also express an indirect command.

(78) a. *dàv= 'ʔyə́de*
F^cc^3=heed
He should listen!

b. *kèr ʔñowi hín dàv= 'cʔį́ʔmi kàr gošthi*
xcs2 companion NEG F^cc^3=pinch xcs door
Your sibling! [I hope] that s/he doesn't get caught in the door!

The three future-tense prefixes illustrated thus far encode events located near the deictic center. The remaining two future-tense prefixes denote person-of-subject and future tense, where future tense views a situation as anticipated or intended, away from the deictic center. There is no first-person prefix in this subset because the first person is, by definition, assumed to be at the deictic center, and the excentric second-person future prefix of this subset is, in fact, homophonous with the first-person future-tense prefix, as can be seen in (71c). To specify the location of an action as excentric when a first-person future prefix is used, a first-order locational prefix is used with it.

The two excentric prefixes of this subset are used in both statements and questions, as in (79), and in injunctions, as in (80). The prefix *dù-* (excentric third-person future) is found in some narrative contexts where the eventline-clause is completive, as in the purpose clause of (79b).

(79) a. *kháʔmɨ pé gù= 'tonci ya*
when? again F^xc^2=go^over now
When are you coming over here again?

b. *bìv= 'ma ya dù= 'hą̣ yɨ̀ hmę̣́ pa gwà= 'ci-he*
C^3=go now F^xc^3=bring cc₂p corncake so IR^1-eat-px
Then she went to bring the corncakes for us to eat.

---

[12]The various forms of the motion verb *ma* 'go' may have inceptive force when used as an auxiliary.

c. *ší-∅ᵥ= 'ma dù= 'ʔwį̨n kɨ̀ ndą̨ni kàr mɔdi*
EL-C^3=go F^xc^3=feed xcp cattle xcs cowherd
The cowherd has gone to feed the cattle.

(80) a. *gù= 'hą̆ cɨ nɨ́, ya š-k-ríᵥ= 'ma nɨ́*
F^xc^2=bring little cc_2 now EL-P^2-DUR=go cc_2
Bring me a little bit from there, since you're going there.

b. *hín gù= 'de*
NEG F^xc^2=delay
Don't stay there a long time.

c. *dàᵥ= 'ma dù= 'šiH kà ʔná dù= 'ʔę̨H cɨ*
F^cc^3=go F^xc^3=tell REL one F^xc^3=come please cc_1
He's going there to tell that one (person) to please come here.

d. *hín dù= 'həH kɨ̀ šithæ*
NEG F^xc^3=fall xcp plank
May those planks (over there) not fall down!

4
Conjunct Second-order Prefixes

Conjunct second-order prefixes are like their primary counterparts in being able to occur alone on verbs without other prefixes. They differ from primary prefixes, however, in failing to fully ground the clauses in which they occur and, therefore, normally occur in dependent clauses and reference spatial or temporal location relative to that of the deictic center of an associated independent clause. Whereas primary prefixes distinguish three tense-aspects (present, completive, future), conjunct prefixes distinguish only two—SIMULTANEOUS and SEQUENTIAL. Rather than directly marking the temporal reference of independent clauses, they mark the situation named by a dependent clause as being simultaneous with that of an associated independent clause or as in sequence with it. Person-of-subject is also marked in each conjunct prefix, and deictic categories in relation to the deictic center and an aspectual distinction between completive and incompletive contexts are also differentially encoded in some conjunct prefixes. The thirteen second-order, conjunct prefixes are presented in (81).

(81) a. *dá-* (SM^1, simultaneous first-person)
gà- (SQ^cc^1, sequential centric first-person)
dí- (SQ^xc^1, sequential excentric first-person)

b. *gá-* (SM^cc^2, simultaneous centric second-person)
búy- (SM^xc^2, simultaneous excentric second-person)
gày- (SQ^cc_1^2, sequential centric$_1$ second-person)
díy- (SQ^cc_2^2, sequential centric$_2$ second-person)
gíy- (SQ^xc^2, sequential excentric second-person)

c. *gàn-* (SM^cc^I^3, simultaneous centric incompletive third-person)
gán- (SM^cc^C^3, simultaneous centric completive third-person)
bú- (SM^xc^3, simultaneous excentric third-person)
dív- (SQ^I^3, sequential incompletive third-person)
gív- (SQ^C^3, sequential completive third-person)

As a cursory glance at the conjunct prefixes listed in (81) indicates, there is a great deal of assymetry in the distinctions which various subsets of prefixes make. While all conjunct prefixes distinguish simultaneous and sequential events as well as the three persons-of-subject, up to three categories of deixis seem only to be distinguished in one triplet of prefixes and the distinction between completive and incompletive aspect is made in a similarly uneven way. These distinctions are discussed in sections that follow after a brief sketch of the syntactic contexts in which conjunct clauses occur.

4.1. The syntactic distribution of conjunct clauses. A complete statement of the use of conjunct clauses would require a thorough analysis and description of Otomí discourse structure. This is clearly beyond the scope of this study. In general terms, however, a conjunct clause (one that has a conjunct prefix in the verb) is dependent upon one or more primary clauses (that have a primary prefix in the verb) occurring in the immediate context. Broadly speaking, conjunct clauses have an adverbial relationship to the matrix clause on which they depend. A few specific syntactic contexts in which conjunct clauses are found are given here, but the reader must be aware that certain illustrations of conjunct clauses throughout this study may have been drawn out of a larger context in such a way that the reason for its occurrence in conjunct form is not readily apparent.

Two syntactic contexts in which conjunct clauses commonly occur are when, in two adjacent clauses, (a) both reference the same real-world subject or (b) the object of the primary clause is also the subject of the conjunct clause.

Coreferential subjects in primary and conjunct clauses are illustrated in (82). In (82a), two primary clauses with *gù-* (first-person future) are conjoined, and a conjunct clause with *dá-* (simultaneous first-person) occurs between them as dependent to the second. In (82b), a primary clause with *gúy-* (second-person completive) is followed by two conjunct clauses with *gíy-* (sequential excentric second-person).

(82) a. *khà gù='mæ-gɔ-ʔbe, wǎ dá='ko-ʔbe gù='ma hanti-ʔbe kàr*
? F^1=go^d-1-dx or SM^1=return-dx F^1=go see-dx

ʔmædi
lost^thing
Shall you and I go on or, going back, shall we look for the lost one?

b. *gúy='ma gíy='koH pɨ̀ her ngų pɨ̀ habɨ gíy='ʔñ*
C^2=go SQ^xc^2=return xc at^2 house xc where? SQ^xc^2=come
You went, returning to your house, whence you had come.

The sentences of (83) illustrate primary clauses whose objects are coreferential with subjects of associated conjunct clauses. In (83a), the direct object of the primary clause, encoded by the suffix *-y* (third-person), is coreferential with the subject of the following conjunct clause with prefix *gán-* (simultaneous centric completive third-person). In (83b), the direct object of the primary clause, encoded by *-gi* (first-person), is coreferential with the subject of the following conjunct clause with prefix *dá-* (simultaneous first-person).

(83) a. *bìv='gų-y gán='ma nɨ́*
C^3=chase-3 SM^cc^C^3=go cc_2
She chased it and it went over there.

b. *ší-∅v='hyànti-gi dá='ʔęhę*
EL-C^3=see-1 SM^1=come
She saw me coming.

In narrative or conversation, when a primary clause is immediately followed by one or more conjunct clauses that are coferential as to subject, the clauses usually encode a sequence of related actions by the named agent. In such sentences, both the primary clause and the conjunct clauses belong to the eventline. When the primary verb is a verb of motion, the conjunct verb encodes a change in both time and location from that of the deictic center.

Conjunct clauses regularly occur as the nominalized or adverbial constituent of an independent clause. The syntactic relation of the conjunct clauses illustrated in (82) and (83), for example, may be considered adverbial. Two further illustrations of conjunct clauses as adverbials follow in (84).

(84) a. *ʔbɨ̀ mí-∅='čʔɨ, hį mí-∅='pɨnte. gá$_n$='hyæH*
when IMPF-P^3=small NEG IMPF-P^3=butt SM^cc^C^3=quit

kí ʔba ya, bì$_v$='mɨdi bì$_v$='pɨnte
xcp3 milk now C^3=begin C^3=butt
When he was small, he did not butt people. But when he was weaned, then he began to butt.

b. *ngų̌ dá='ʔwege-he pɨ̀ hár ngų kàr čuhču ʔbɨ́,*
like SM^1=leave-px xc at^3 house xcs old^lady then

ya ʔbɨ̀ n-dú='ʔəde-he ya, ʔįną, ya š-kí$_v$='dų́
now then IMPF-C^1=hear-px now say now EL-SQ^C^3=die
It seems as though we left the the old lady's house then. And then when we heard (about her), they said she had died.

Conjunct clauses also occur in a variety of ways as nominal constituents of clauses. Stative verbs, for example, commonly take a conjunct clause as subject, as in (85).

(85) a. *∅=rá$_n$-'mpa gà$_n$='mbəH kàr dehe*
P^3=ST-hot SM^cc^I^3=come^out xcs water
The water comes out hot.

b. *∅=rá$_n$-'nthį gà$_n$='nįgi to gì$_y$='tɔti gì$_y$='*
P^3=ST-hard SM^cc^I^3=appear who? F^cc^2=find F^cc^2=talk-d
It is difficult for you to find someone with whom to talk.

c. *m-∅=rá$_n$-cí-'zɔ n-gá$_n$='šɔdi*
IMPF-P^3=ST-great-good IMPF-SM^cc^C^3=sing
He used to sing beautifully.

In (86a), a conjunct clause functions as postposed relative-clause modifier to a noun and, in (86b), two conjunct clauses provide expanded subject reference to an initial primary clause.

(86) a. *kàr angel, ʔbɨ́, bì$_v$='hñįni ∅=rá$_n$-'ngeH kí dæthą kà*
xcs Angel then C^3=sick P^3=ST-be xcp3 corn REL

š-ká$_n$='pošti
EL-SM^cc^C^3=black
Then Angel became ill on account of their corn that turned black.

b. *dú=ˈmɔh-me, ʔbɨ́, kɨ̀ to n-dá=ˈyoh-me, kɨ̀*
C^1=go^p-px then xcp who? IMPF-SM^1=accompany-px xcp

n-dá=ˈpa-gɔ
IMPF-SM^1=go-1
We went then, we who were travelling together.

Conjunct clauses also regularly occur after certain adverbs. The common occurrence of conjunct clauses as nominals suggests a syntactic analysis with preposed adverb in which the adverb is a predicate or topic with the conjunct clause as subject or comment. They often (but not always) occur, for example, with the negative word *hin* or the negative imperative word *ʔyó*, as illustrated in (87) and (88).

(87) a. *nuke, hin gí$_y$=ˈʔį̨ni. hį́ną-gɔ, hin dá=ˈʔį̨n-gɔ. dú=ˈma*
2 NEG SQ^xc^2=play NEG-1 NEG SM^1=play-1 C^1=go

kʔąhti-ki-tho-hɨ
see-2-AFF-p
You; you didn't play. Not me; I didn't play. I went and just watched you (pl).

b. *mí-∅=ˈših-mɨ pé ∅-dì$_v$=ˈyohpi ∅-dì$_v$=ˈnšaha.*
IMPF-P^3=tell-p again P^3-DURir^C=repeat P^3-DURir^C=bathe now

hin gá$_n$=ˈne kàr bąhci
NEG SM^cc^C^3=want xcs child
They told him to bathe a second time, but the child did not want to do it.

(88) a. *ʔyó dí$_y$=ˈntųhni-wi*
NEG! SQ^cc$_2$^2=fight-d
Don't you two fight!

b. *mí-∅=ˈhɨti pa dà$_v$=ˈʔyəH nɨ̀r khąʔnį. dà$_v$=ˈʔyəde; ʔyó*
IMPF-P^3=whip so F^cc^3=heed ccs person F^cc^3=heed NEG!

dí$_v$=ˈntųhni
SQ^I^3=fight
They used to whip them so that they would take heed. Let him take heed! Let him not keep fighting.

Some of the other adverbs that are commonly followed by a conjunct clause are *há* 'how?' in an indirect question (89a), *cín* 'early, quickly' (89b), *ngetiką* 'quickly' (89c), and *ʔdàʔcɨ* 'gradually' (89d).

(89) a. *nɨ̀r cuento dige kàr mphɨnci, há dá='phɨnci, há*
ccs story about xcs fall how? SM^1=fall how?

gán='ʔyenti-gi nɨ̀m phani-he
SM^cc^C^3=knock^down-1 ccs1 horse-px
This is the story about the fall, how I fell, how our (ex) horse knocked me down.

b. *khà cín gíy='nanci mą́-nšudi ndomngo*
? early SQ^xc^2=arise former-morning Sunday
Did you get up early last Sunday morning?

c. *ngetiką gàn='mbɨnci yɨ̀ pa*
quickly SM^cc^I^3=roll^over ccp day
The days go by quickly.

d. *ʔdàʔcɨ ʔdàʔcɨ gán='šɔh-ki ya kàr cʔi-chį*
gradual gradual SM^cc^C^3=teach-1 now xcs pulque-drinking
Gradually, then, he taught me to drink pulque.

Less commonly, a nominal may initiate a clause with following conjunct clause as its partner in what would appear to be a topic-comment syntax, as in (90).

(90) a. *cǽ-the gàn='mpeni yɨ̀ khąʔnį*
cold-water SM^cc^I^3=wash ccp person
In cold water these people wash clothes.

b. *cincuenta gn-wà='mɔ ʔnàr manga, ʔną́*
fifty SM^cc^I^3-PRG^I=sell one^in sarape say
For fifty pesos they sell a blanket (in the market), they say.

In the next three sections, each of the subsets of conjunct prefixes listed in (18) is illustrated and discussed in detail.

4.2. First-person conjunct prefixes. There are only three first-person conjunct prefixes. This is probably an artifact of the pragmatics of the speech situation, where the first person is normally found at the deictic center at deictic center time. There is thus a single prefix *dá-* (simultaneous first-person) to denote simultaneous events for first-person subjects, whether the context is completive or incompletive. In order to specifically portray a first-person to be located away from the deictic center, deictic adverbs or adverbial phrases are used.

(91) a. *∅-bà= 'hæ-gi-tho dá= 'ʔę̨hę̨*
P^3-PRG^1=allow-1-AFF SM^1=come
She allows me to come (here).

b. *khà gù= 'mæ-gɔ-ʔbe, wǎ dá= 'ko-ʔbe gù= 'ma hanti-ʔbe kàr*
? F^1=go^d-1-dx or SM^1=return-dx F^1=go see-dx

ʔmædi
lost^thing
Shall you and I go on or, going back, shall we look for the lost one?

c. *gí= 'tų̨nthų̨, khą̨ nùgɔ dá= 'niñą̨-tho*
P^2=hunger and 1 SM^1=satiated-AFF
You are hungry, and I have eaten to the full.

d. *dú= 'ma dá= 'koH pɨ̀ hám ngų̨ pɨ̀ habɨ dá= 'ʔę̨hę̨*
C^1=go SM^1=return xc at^1 house xc at SM^1=come
I went, returning to my house from which I came.

To denote sequential events, there are two first-person prefixes which distinguish distance (space or time) from the deictic center. The first of these is the prefix *gà-* (sequential centric first-person) which denotes a first-person sequential event at the deictic center. It occurs only in incompletive contexts. The full phonological form of this prefix is never actually attested, since it is always found with a first-order prefix which triggers the loss of its vowel and tone. I propose the underlying form *gà-* entirely on analogy with *$gà_y$-* (sequential $centric_1$ second-person).

(92) a. *mæ̌ g-rá= 'kʔą̨ʔti-wi*
go^di SQ^cc^1-PNC^cc=see-di
Let's you and I go see them.

b. *há g-rá= 'šìʔ-ki hmą̨́*
how? SQ^cc^1-PNC^cc=tell-2 FRUSTRATIVE
How can I explain it to you?

The second sequential first-person prefix is *dí-* (sequential excentric first-person) which denotes an event away from the deictic center. This prefix may occur in either incompletive or completive contexts.

(93) a. *te dí='hon-gɔ-wi, mehor gù='mæ dí='ʔo-bi*
in P^1=seek-1-di better F^1=go^d SQ^xc^1=go^to^bed-di
What do we want (here)? It is better that we (two) go (home) and go to bed.

b. *ʔeške dú='ma dí='thɨti ʔnęhę*
EMPH C^1=go SQ^xc^1=burn also
Right away I went and burned them, too.

c. *nuya, sta dú='cɨdi-he, ya dí='cɨdi-he pɨ hâr*
now until C^1=overtake-px now SQ^xc^1=overtake-px xc at^s

tʔɔ̌
mountain
So, it was then that we overtook (her). We overtook (her) there at the mountain.

4.3. Second-person conjunct prefixes. There are five second-person conjunct prefixes. Two of them denote simultaneous events, also encoding two degrees of distance from the deictic center. The first of these is the prefix *gá-* (simultaneous centric second-person), which addresses a second-person near the speaker. It occurs in both incompletive and completive contexts, but more often than not occurs with a third-order prefix.

(94) a. *menta gá='tæni-hɨ nɨr ʔñų, hin gìy='ʔmædi-hɨ*
while SM^cc^2=follow-p ccs road NEG F^cc^2=lost-p
As long as you follow this road, you will not get lost.

b. *dú='nzoʔ-ki ʔbɨ̀ ya šì n-gá='thógi*
C^1=call-2 when now EL IMPF-SM^cc^2=pass
I called you when you were passing by.

c. *nuya, ya š-kú= 'ʔñəthe rán- 'ngu̜, khà gí= 'cɔ, ya*
now now EL-C^2=medicate ST-much ? P^2=feel now

š-ká= 'zɔ
EL-SM^cc^2=recover
Now that you've taken medicine for quite a long time, do you feel that you are getting better?

The second simultaneous second-person prefix is *búy-* (simultaneous excentric second-person), which addresses a second-person at a distance from the speaker.[13] This prefix usually has imperative force. Because of its excentric reference, it entails inbound motion, towards the deictic center.

(95) a. *búy= 'ʔe̜he̜ š-k-rì= 'ʔbɨ̀p-hɨ wa*
SM^xc^2=come EL-F^cc^2-DURir^I=be-p cc_1
Come and we can be together over here.

b. *búy= 'hña̜ cɨ kàr thu̜hni̜*
SM^xc^2=bring please xcs chair
Please bring the chair.

The remaining three second-person prefixes denote that events occur sequentially in relation to other events in the context. They are unusual among prefixes in distinguishing three degrees of deixis in relation to the deictic center. Whereas adverbs and noun phrases distinguish three deictic categories, verb prefixes ordinarily do not. These prefixes are further anomalous in the way they occur in respect to aspect: the two centric prefixes only occur in incompletive contexts, whereas the excentric prefix occurs most often in completive contexts but is also occasionally found in incompletive contexts.

The first of these prefixes is *gày-* (sequential centric$_1$ second-person). It is used as a command, with centric$_1$ force making the injunction direct and unsoftened. The addressee is told to act immediately, right at the deictic center.

(96) a. *ʔeš š-kày= 'ʔyæni ya kàr da̜htu̜ pa gìy- 'pɔh-ki*
EMPH EL-SQ^cc_1^2=measure now xcs cloth so F^cc^2-sell-1
Measure the cloth right away so you can sell it to me.

---

[13]There is at least one exception in the use of this prefix in which the palatal augment is absent in second person with the verb *ʔe̜he̜* 'come'. Further research is required to resolve this issue.

b. *ʔeš š-kà$_y$= 'hñą̆ši nɨ̀r thǽgi, g-rí$_v$= 'thoH nɨ́r*
EMPH EL-SQ^cc_1^2=take cc_2s saw F^cc^2-DUR=pass cc_2s3 house

kàr berto
xcs Robert
Take the saw right away and go past Robert's house.

The second sequential second-person prefix is *dí$_y$-* (sequential centric$_2$ second-person) and may also be used in direct commands and in indirect commands as the complement of a speech verb. As such a complement, it can occur in a completive context; but otherwise it only occurs in an incompletive context. The force of the centric$_2$ denotation softens this prefix when used as a command. It is not always a command, however, and may merely denote that a second-person eventline situation is incompletive.

(97) a. *gì$_y$= 'mă dí$_y$= 'cì kèr ʔñį́thį*
F^cc^2=go SQ^cc_2^2=eat xcs2 medicine
Go take your medicine.

b. *sá, ngų̆ dú= 'šiʔ-ki dí$_y$= 'ʔñįh kwa, ʔně hį š-kú= 'ʔįhį*
hmph! as C^1=tell-2 SQ^cc_2^2=come cc_1 but NEG EL-C^2=come
Hmph! It seems I told you to come here, but you did not come.

c. *š-tí$_y$= 'tų̀-gé*
EL-SQ^cc_2^2=die-2
You will die (sometime).

The third sequential second-person prefix is *gí$_y$-* (sequential excentric second-person). It differs from the other two sequential second-person prefixes in denoting an excentric location. As indicated above, it occurs most often in completive contexts, but it is also occasionally found in incompletive contexts. Unlike *dí$_y$-* (sequential centric$_2$ second-person), it is used in statements and questions and does not have imperative force.

(98) a. *khà cín gí$_y$= 'nanci mą́-nšudi ndomngo*
? early SQ^xc^2=arise former-morning Sunday
Did you get up early last Sunday morning?

b. *to bú= 'ʔdaʔ-ki kà gí$_y$= 'ci ya ʔbɨ́*
who? SM^xc^3=give-2 REL SQ^xc^2=consume now then
Who gave you [the liquor] you consumed at that time?

c. *gú= 'ma gí_y= 'koH pɨ̀ her ngų pɨ̀ habɨ gí*
C^2=go SQ^xc^2=return xc at^2 house xc where? SQ^xc^2=come
You went, returning to your house, whence you had come.

d. *nuke, hin gí_y= 'ʔįni. hįną-gɔ, hin dá= 'ʔįn-gɔ. dú= 'ma*
2 NEG SQ^xc^2=play NEG-1 NEG SM^1=play-1 C^1=go

kʔąhti-ki-tho-hɨ
see-2-AFF-p
You; you didn't play. Not me; I didn't play. I went and just watched you (pl).

e. *ʔbɨ̀ gì_y= 'cí nɨ̀r ʔñį́thį́, š-kí_y= 'zɔ, ʔb*
when F^cc^2=eat ccs medicine EL-SQ^xc^2=get^well then
If you take this medicine, you will get well then.

4.4. Third-person conjunct prefixes. There are five third-person conjunct prefixes, three to mark events as simultaneous with the events of related verbs and two to mark them as occurring in sequence with related events. The three simultaneous prefixes distinguish deictic reference as centric or excentric, the two centric prefixes further distinguish incompletive from completive aspect.

In (99), the prefix *gà_n-* (simultaneous centric incompletive third-person) is illustrated.

(99) a. *∅=rá_n- 'nthį gà_n= 'nįgi to gì_y= 'tɔti gì_y= '*
P^3=ST-hard SM^cc^I^3=appear who? F^cc^2=find F^cc^2=talk-d
It is difficult for you to find someone with whom to talk.

b. *dí= 'mąn-gɔ kɨ̀ mįngų san felipe cin gà_n= 'ndù-hɨ*
P^1=say-1 xcp inhabitant Saint Philip early SM^cc^I^3=die-p
I say that the inhabitants of San Felipe die early.

c. *cǽ-the gà_n= 'mpěni yɨ̀ khą̀ʔnį*
cold-water SM^cc^I^3=wash ccp person
It is in cold water that these people wash clothes.

In (100), the prefix *gá_n-* (simultaneous centric completive third-person) is illustrated.

(100) a. *khà nkhwąnį ge? pi gán= 'nzəH pi mą́nde*
? truly be xc SM^cc^C^3=arrive^here xc yesterday
Is that truly where s/he arrived yesterday?

b. *bì$_{v}$= 'ma gán= 'ngoH pi hár ngų pi habi*
C^3=go SM^cc^C^3=return xc at^3 house xc where?

g$_{v}$-wí= '?ñęhę
SQ^C^3-PNCxc=come
He returned to his house whence he had come.

c. *bì$_{v}$= 'gų-y gán= 'ma ní*
C^3=chase-3 SM^cc^C^3=go cc_2
She chased it and it went over there.

d. *?bì mí-∅= 'č?i, hį mí-∅= 'pinte. gán= 'hyæH kí*
when IMPF-P^3=small NEG IMPF-P^3=butt SM^cc^C^3=quit xcp3

?ba ya, bì$_{v}$= 'midi bì$_{v}$= 'pinte
milk now C^3=begin C^3=butt
When he was small, he did not butt people. But when he was weaned, then he began to butt.

In (101), the prefix *bú-* (simultaneous excentric third-person) is illustrated. Although this prefix seems always to be found in completive aspect contexts, there does not appear to be an incompletive prefix that specifically contrasts with it while also marking simultaneous excentric third-person. The prefix *dù-* (excentric third-person future) tends to occur in contexts where such a prefix might be expected.

(101) a. *bú=?nà- 'k?ą ya kár macho kí sario*
SM^xc^3=sudden-appear now xcs3 mule xcp3 Cesario
Then from over there suddenly the mule of Cesario's family appeared (from behind something).

b. *kàr karro kà gán= 'mɔh-mi, pé bú= 'tə-ti-hi ?bì*
xcs bus REL SM^cc^C^3=go^p-p again SM^xc^3=ride-AFF-p when

m-bú= 'koh-mi
IMPF-SM^xc^3=return-p
That bus that they went on is (the one) they took again when they came back.

c. *pɨ̀ hábɨ dú= 'má bú= 'həš-ki ʔmį̣nį̣*
xc at C^1=go SM^xc^3=fall^on-1 pricker
There where I went, prickers fell all over me.

The two third-person sequential prefixes distinguish incompletive and completive contexts, but distance from the deictic center is not explicitly contrasted. In (102), the prefix *dí$_v$-* (sequential incompletive third-person) is illustrated. This prefix may be obsolescent; very few, and only older speakers seem to use it. Its completive counterpart *gí$_v$-* (sequential completive third-person) is illustrated in (103).

(102) a. *gì$_y$=ndo- 'ʔyɔ̀h-pi kàokhą̆, dí$_v$= 'ʔñą́n-ti nìr bą̀hci*
F^cc^2=greatly-ask-BEN God SQ^I^3=move-AFF ccs2 child
Urgently ask God. Your child will live.

b. *dí$_v$= 'ʔbɔH pɨ̀ kàr thų̣hnį̣, š-tá= 'kɨʔti*
SQ^I^3=stand xc xcs chair EL-SM^1=put^in
Let the chair stand there; I'll put it inside.

c. *dú= 'šiH kàr nąną dà$_v$= 'má d-rí$_v$= 'ʔun k*
C^1=tell xcs older^woman F^cc^3=go SQ^I^3-DUR=give xcs

ʔñį̣thį̣ pɨ̀ hár ngų
medicine xc at^3 house
I told the woman to go and give him/her the medicine there at her house.

d. *khą̀ kɨ̀ ší-Ø$_v$= 'ndų́, solamente kàokhą̆ ʔì= 'pą̆di hábɨ*
and xcp EL-P^3=die only God P^3=know where?

dí$_v$= 'zǐci
SQ^I^3=take
And those who have died, only God knows where he will take them.

(103) a. *bì$_v$= 'gɨ̀ ɨ̀r ʔdihi kàr khąʔñį, bì$_v$= 'dæn kàr metrio,*
C^3=take^hold ins run xcs person C^3=follow xcs Demetrio

bì$_v$= 'ma gí$_v$= 'zɨdi nɨ̀ rá= 'khă nɨ́
C^3=go SQ^C^3=overtake cc$_2$ PNCcc=make cc$_2$
That person broke into a run; he followed Demetrio; he went, and overtook him over there.

b. *bì$_v$= 'ma gí$_v$= 'ʔmɔ hâr thi*
C^3=go SQ^C^3=stand^still at^s yard
He went and stood still in the yard.

c. *bì$_v$= 'ma gá$_n$= 'ngoH pɨ̀ hár ngų pɨ̀ habɨ*
C^3=go SM^cc^C^3=return xc at^3 house xc where?

g$_v$-wí= 'ʔñęhę
SQ^C^3-PNCxc=come
He returned to his house whence he had come.

5
Third-order Prefixes

With the presentation of second-order prefixes, which are always present in the Otomí verb, we may now proceed to the discussion of third-order prefixes, which function temporally and appear in both main and subordinate clauses. The three third-order prefixes are listed in (104).

(104) *mí-* (imperfect)
má- (imperfect)
ší- (eventline)

The imperfect prefixes are discussed first (§§5.1–3), followed by the eventline prefix (§§5.4–5).

5.1. The imperfect prefixes. The prefixes *mí-* and *má-* encode imperfect aspect. As indicated in the phonological discussion (§1.7), *mí-* is usually reduced phonologically to *m-*, *n-*, or *w-* when followed by most second- or third-order prefixes, the primary exception being its occurrence alone with the zero form of the third-person present-tense prefix, where it appears in its full phonological form. Each of these phonological forms of *mí-* is illustrated in (105a)–(105d).

(105) a. *mí-∅=ndo-'dehpe-tho* *yɨ̀* *mbaškhwa*
IMPF-P^3=greatly-spend^time-AFF cc_2p fiesta
They used to spend a lot of time in religious fiestas.

b. *m-Ø-bá='ʔdacæ* *m-Ø-bá='ʔo* *kàr ʔñụ*
IMPF-P^3-PRG^C=alone IMPF-P^3-PRG^C=be^in xcs road
She was going along by herself in the road.

c. *n-dí='təʔ-pi* *kár phani kàr elihio*
IMPF-P^1=ride-BEN xcs3 horse xcs Eligio
I used to ride Eligio's horse.

d. *nuke hín gwí='ci* *chị*
2 NEG IMPF^P^2=drink pulque
You didn't used to drink pulque.

The imperfect prefix may also be realized as *má-*, which always occurs in third-person present-tense clauses which are off the eventline as collateral information, and frequently in motion verbs, as in *má-Ø='ʔbæto* 's/he was going along ahead'. Although *má-* (imperfect) can occur with the eventline adverb *šĩ-* in main clauses that are synchronous with but collateral to the eventline, it is also commonly found in subordinate clauses.

(106) a. *ʔbɨ̀* *mí_v='zəti-wi* *má-Ø='tu-wi* *kàr šiphani*
when IMPF^C^3=arrive^there-d IMPF-P^3=carry-d xcs pigskin
When the two arrived, they were carrying the pigskin (agave-wine bottle).

b. *kɨ̀ tó mí-Ø='honi ya, ʔbɨ́, ya šĩ má-Ø='pa,*
xcp in IMPF-P^3=seek now when now EL IMPF-P^3=go

má-Ø='serka-hɨ dìgè hábɨ m-Ø-rá='ʔbæn kạ́
IMPF-P^3=approach-p REL where? IMPF-P^3-PNC^cc=lie xcs
The ones who were looking for him, then, at that point were getting near the place where he was lying.

c. *hị n-dí='pǡdi hábɨ gèʔ pɨ̀ g-rá='kɨti ya,*
NEG IMPF-P^1=know where? be xc F^1-PNC^cc=enter now

pe má-Ø='ʔbætó tó kạ̀ m-Ø-rá='gía-gi
but IMPF-P^3=go^ahead in xcs IMPF-P^3-PNC^cc=guide-1
I did not know where I was going to go in, but the person who was guiding me was going ahead.

d. *mí-Ø='pa yɨ̀ ʔbǽhñą̀, má-Ø='khò phòphàní,*
IMPF-P^3=go cc₂p woman IMPF-P^3=gather manure

m-Ø=rán-ndò-'ką-di ndą́ni ʔbɨ́
IMPF-P^3=ST-great-be^p-AFF cattle when
The women used to go; they used to gather manure; there used to be a great many cattle then.

e. *kàr ndą́ni mí-Ø='pɨ̌šti, má-Ø='héhk-hɨ kɨ̀ ngǒ*
xcs cow IMPF-P^3=skin IMPF-P^3=divide-p xcp meat
They were skinning the cow and dividing up the meat.

f. *kàr burro hín gán='nzų́, bì='gą̀ti, ya š*

xcs donkey NEG SM^cc^C^3=fear C^3=go^down^into now EL

má-Ø=pa màdě kàr dą̀the
IMPF-P^3=go middle xcs river
The donkey was not afraid. He went down into the river; at that time he was just going in the middle of the river.

g. *ʔbɨ̀ mí-Ø='zəti-wi, má-Ø='tų̌-wi kàr šìphàní,*
when IMPF-P^3=arrive^d IMPF-P^3=carry-d xcs pulque^skin

ya téngų̌-tho má-Ø='po
now little-AFF IMPF-P^3=contain
When the two who were carrying the pulque skin arrived at the field, it had only a little bit in it.

h. *mientra má-Ø='thóH kɨ̀ khěya, n-gn-wá='ʔmɨ̀H*
while IMPF-P^3=pass xcp year IMPF-SM^cc^C^3-PRG^C=born xcp
As the years passed, they were born.

The full form of *má-* only occurs in examples like those given above—those with the zero form of the third-person present-tense prefix alone. In this context, *mí-* would appear to occur in eventline verbs, *má-* in verbs off the eventline. The presence of any other second- or third-order prefix would reduce *má-* to the same phonological forms *m-*, *n-*, and *w-* that result from the combining of *mí-* with such prefixes. It is, therefore, impossible to make any claim about there being any more than one imperfect prefix in such contexts, in the absence of phonological features to distinguish the two prefixes in these contexts, either for speaker or for analyst. In the remainder of this study, therefore, the imperfect prefix will be referred to generally as *mí-*, and nothing further will be said of *má-* as a separate prefix occurring in contexts other than alone with *∅* (third-person present).

The imperfect prefix may occur with either primary or conjunct second-order prefixes. The combinations that may occur and their semantic force are described in the following two sections.

5.2. Imperfect *mí-* with primary second-order prefixes. Imperfect occurs with both present tense and completive aspect, but is semantically incompatible with future tense, with the result that third-order *mí-* (imperfect) does not occur together in the same verb with a second-order future-tense prefix.

Present imperfect. With present tense, the imperfect prefix references an incomplete state or continuing event in the past, i.e., prior to immediate eventline time and without reference to the beginning or end of the state or event. The reading of the present tense in this context may be considered habitual or continuous, without reference to position on the timeline, with imperfect focusing upon the incompleteness of the event and anchoring it to a span in past time. Imperfect *mí-* may occur with any of the three present-tense prefixes, but only with the zero form of the third-person present. These combinations are illustrated in (107).

(107) a. *ʔbɨ̀ n-dí='čʔɨ, n-dí='pæʔci ngṵ̌ yohto kheyæ,*
when IMPF-P^1=small IMPF-P^1-have like seven year

n-dí='ʔbɨ̀ʔ-ʔbe kàm tio
IMPF-P^1-be-dx xcs1 uncle
When I was small, when I was about seven years old, I was living with my uncle.

b. *nuke n-gí=ndo-'ʔa̰ha̰*
2 IMPF-P2=great-sleep
You were sound asleep.

c. *mí-∅='pa̰ha̰ kàr ʔñḭthḭ*
IMPF-P^3=smell xcs medicine
S/he used to smell the insecticide.

d. *dú= 'nkəni hín dwí= 'meya-ki*
C^1=deny NEG IMPF^P^1=know-2
I denied that I knew you.

Completive imperfect. The imperfect prefix occurs with completive prefixes only in conditional or temporal subordinate clauses, usually introduced by *ʔbɨ̀* 'when, then'.[14] This combination of prefixes marks the situation encoded in the subordinate clause as occurring during or simultaneous with the situation encoded by the independent clause. The three completive prefixes are illustrated with imperfect in (108).

(108) a. *ʔbɨ̀ n-dú= 'pəH pɨ̀ ha-m ngų,*
when IMPF-C^1=come^out xc at-1 house

m-∅-bá= 'ʔą-tho kàm bą̀hci
IMPF-P^3-PRG^C=sleep-AFF xcs^1 child
When I came out of my house, my child was still sleeping.

b. *dí= 'ʔɔn-ki habɨ gíᵧ= 'cəh-ke ʔbɨ̀ n-gú= 'ʔñęH*
P^1=ask-2 where? SQ^xc^2=arrive^here-2 when IMPF-C^2=come

ʔmundɔ
Mexico
I ask you, where did you arrive when you came from Mexico City?

c. *mą́nde ʔbɨ̀ n-gú= 'cəhə, š-kíᵧ=ndò- 'ntį́*
yesterday when IMPF-C^2=arrive^here EL-SQ^xc^2=greatly-drunk
Yesterday when you arrived here, you were very drunk.

d. *ʔbɨ̀ míᵥ= 'zɨ hųšadi ya, bɨ̀ᵥ= 'nkha ʔnàr gų*
when IMPF^C^3=reach noon now C^3=appear one^in cloud
At noon, a cloud appeared.

5.3. Imperfect *mí-* with conjunct second-order prefixes. SIMULTANEOUS, the conjunct category that corresponds to the primary category PRESENT, is the only one that occurs together in the same verb with IMPERFECT. SEQUENTIAL and IRREALIS prefixes may not so occur.

---

[14]When phonological reshaping of *mí-* (imperfect) with *bɨ̀ᵥ-* (third-person completive) to *míᵥ-* occurs in the speech of older speakers, they frequently omit *ʔbɨ̀* 'when' from the conditional clause in which it occurs.

When simultaneous and imperfect occur together, they have the same force as when present and imperfect occur together, the difference being primarily the syntactic position of the conjunct clause. Of the six simultaneous prefixes, however, only three occur with imperfect, because in this context they only distinguish the three persons-of-subject, without other semantic distinctions being made. The three that occur in this context are *dá-* (simultaneous first-person), *gá-* (simultaneous centric second-person), and *gá*$_n$- (simultaneous centric completive third-person).

(109) a. *n-dá=ˈma n-dá=ˈʔàni, hį n-dá=ˈhɔti kɨ̀*
IMPF-SM^1=go IMPF-SM^1=stoop NEG IMPF-SM^1=endure xcp wood
I used to go along stooped over, unable to bear (the weight of) the wood.

b. *te ɨ̀r ʔbæʔ ką n-gá=ˈmą-mi ʔbɨ̀ n-gá=ˈʔño-wi*
what? ins thing xcs IMPF-SM^cc^2=say-d when IMPF-SM^cc^2=walk-d

hâr ʔñų
at^s road
What were you two saying as you walked in the road?

c. *pe kàm khwądą, ʔbɨ̀ n-gá*$_n$*=ˈnzəH ya,*
but xcs1 brother when IMPF-SM^cc^C^3=arrive now

mí-∅-ˈʔəde mí-∅=ʔ-ˈcan-gi
IMPF-P^3=hear IMPF-P^3=PASS-scold-1
But my brother, when he used to arrive, he would hear me being scolded.

5.4. The eventline adverb *šì*. Before discussing *ší-* as an eventline prefix, I need to make a disclaimer. As will be seen below, there are two forms, *šì* and *ší-*, which are both glossed as marking a verb as an eventline (EL) verb. Although a full discourse analysis of the role of these forms has not been undertaken, it is clear that their function is slightly different, although related. The low-tone form *šì* is a phonologically separate word which occurs in limited contexts, often followed by an imperfect verb—where *šì* normally precedes the prefix *mí-* (imperfect) or *má-* (imperfect)—or followed by a nonverbal predicate.

(110) a. *kàm dąme ya šì m-∅=ˈɨ́r viudo ką́*
xcs1 husband now EL IMPF-P^3=be widower xcs
My husband was already a widower.

b. *ya šì má-∅='pa made kàr dąthe*
now EL IMPF-P^3=go middle xcs river
He was just then passing in the middle of the river.

c. *gú='nzoh-ki ʔbɨ̀ ya šì n-dá='thogi*
C^2=call-1 when now EL IMPF-SM^1=pass
You called out to me when I was passing by.

d. *ya šì ɨ̀r ánima*
now EL P^3 soul
Now it is a spirit (of a deceased person).

The high-tone form *ší-*, on the other hand, occurs only preceding verbs in the absence of *mí-* (imperfect) and undergoes phonological reduction of the same sort as other verb prefixes.

(111) a. *š-∅-ní$_v$='hmųnci yɨ̀ khąʔnį, š-∅-ní$_v$='nkhà ∅ thɨ*
EL-P^3-DUR=gather cc_2p person EL-P^3-DUR=do inp whistle

š-∅-ní$_v$='nkhà ∅ hmáphi
EL-P^3-DUR=do inp shout
The people are gathering together, there is whistling, there is shouting.

b. *cį š-kí$_y$='khwaH ʔbeni*
quick EL-SQ^xc^2-finish wash^clothes
You finished washing clothes quickly.

And yet, there are a few contexts in which the low-tone form *šì* is also found preceding a verb that is not imperfect. Some of these are illustrated in (112). In these cases, the adverb *šì* occurs in a subordinate clause or as an object complement.

(112) a. *ngų̌ šì gà$_n$='mąn kàm ʔñowi, ∅=rá$_n$-ndo-'nthį*
as EL SM^cc^I^3=say xcs1 companion P^3=ST-greatly-difficult

kèr hñą-hɨ
xcs2 language-p
As my companion says, your (pl) language is very difficult.

b. *ʔbɨ̀ šì bì$_{v}$='nįgi kàr domi, gù='tɔy*
when EL C^3=appear XCS money F^1=buy
When the money appears, I will buy it.

c. *ʔì='nè šì g-rì='thæci*
P^3=want EL F^1=hold
(The baby) wants me to keep holding him.

The adverbial form appears to occur in subordinate situations of one kind or another. Although I do not yet fully understand its distribution, the important point here is that the function of low-tone form *šì* is quite peripheral to this study. With this disclaimer, then, I proceed to the discussion of the high-tone form *ší-* (eventline) and treat it as a third-order prefix.

5.5. The eventline prefix *ší-*. The prefix *ší-* encodes a clause in a narrative, conversation, or exposition as on the eventline or as synchronous with it. Like the imperfect prefix, this prefix may occur with either primary or conjunct second-order prefixes. The combinations that may occur and their semantic force are described in this section, first with primary prefixes and then with conjunct prefixes.

Primary prefixes. All three persons-of-subject and all three tense-aspects are fully compatible with the eventline prefix. The occurrence of the three present-tense prefixes with the eventline prefix is illustrated in (113). Whereas present tense may have a habitual interpretation in other contexts, the presence of *ší-* narrows present-tense reference to a specific point in time and frequently to a specific instance. As (113c) shows, however, a single instance does not imply that an event is instantaneous.

(113) a. *ya š-tí='ʔdaʔ-ki go bæšo yìr zǎ*
now EL-P^1=give-2 four peso CCP2 wood
I'm giving you four pesos for your wood.

b. *ya š-kí=cí-'pąđi ʔnį*
now EL-P2=slightly-know also
You also already know quite a bit.

c. *ya š-kì='ʔan-tho gà$_{n}$='ʔñó*
now EL-P^3=stoop-AFF SM^CC^3=walk
S/he stoops when s/he walks.

Eventline *ší-* may also occur with completive aspect prefixes, as the sentences of (114) show; although a unique phonological form of the third-person completive prefix, usually realized as *bì$_v$-*, is found in this context. Specifically, this second-order prefix is realized solely as the augmenting element $_v$ when following eventline *ší-*.

(114) a. *ya š-tú='tą̱hki Ø=rán-'ngų̱ nɨ̀r thą̱*
now EL-C^1=shell P^3=ST-many cc₂s corn
I have just now shelled a lot of corn.

b. *hį̱ š-kú='yo-ke-wi kèr ta*
NEG EL-C^2=accompany-2-d xcs2 father
You haven't come with your father.

c. *ší-Ø$_v$='ma hmándado, hį̱ Ø-rà='ʔbɨy*
EL-C^3=go errand NEG P^3-PNC^ir=present
She has gone on an errand and is not home.

All five future-tense prefixes occur with the eventline prefix, but only the two third-person forms—centric and excentric—occur alone with the eventline prefix in the absence of a first-order prefix. First- and second-person future forms appear to occur with the eventline prefix only when a first-order prefix is also present. In contexts where first- or second-person future forms might be expected with only the eventline prefix, a conjunct prefix is normally found. The illustrations in (115), therefore, include first-order prefixes; but discussion of these is delayed until §6.

(115) a. *bú='ʔę̱hę̱ š-k-rì='ʔbɨ̀p-hɨ wa*
SM^xc^3=come EL-F^1-DURir=be-pi cc₁
Come here so that we (incl) can be together.

b. *ʔbɨ̀ š-tá='ma, š-k-wá='šiH ya, ʔbɨ́, dù='ʔ*
when EL-SM^1=go EL-F^1-PRG^C=tell now when F^xc^3=come
When I go (there), I'll tell him/her, then, to come (here).

c. *nkháʔmɨ š-k$_y$-wí='ʔñę̱H ʔbɨ́, gì$_y$='zængwa-gi*
sometime EL-F^cc^2-DUR=come when F^cc^2=visit-1
Sometime when you are coming over (from there), visit me.

(116) a. *khóʔci dà$_v$= 'hmunci kɨ̀ zǎ; ya š-tà$_v$= 'hwíti*
move F^cc^3=join xcp wood; now EL-F^cc^3=extinguish

kàr cìbi
xcs fire
Move the firebrands close together; the fire is about to go out.

b. *ya ʔbɨ̀ š-tà$_v$= 'nšudi, mí-∅= 'nanci-hɨ, pé*
now when EL-F^cc^3=morning IMPF-P^3=arise-p again

m-∅-rí$_v$= 'mɔh-mɨ, hâr templo
IMPF-P^3-DUR-go^p-p at^s church
Then when morning would come, they would get up, and then they would go to church.

c. *sta ñòhto ɨ̀r šudi, khą š-tù= 'ʔęH*
until seven ins tomorrow and EL-F^xc^3=come xcs sister
A week from tomorrow the sister will come back.

d. *ʔɔ̀dé, š-tù= 'nų ʔbɨ̀ dù= 'ʔę nonši*
listen EL-F^xc^3=see if F^xc^3=come Monday
Listen! He will decide whether he will come on Monday.

Conjunct prefixes. Simultaneous-event prefixes are illustrated in (117) as they occur with the third-order prefix *ší-* (eventline). When two or more clauses within a sentence contain a prefix string that includes *ší-*, the actions they name are marked as occurring simultaneously.

Of the six simultaneous prefixes, only the four centric ones occur with the eventline prefix. The excentric force of *bú-* and *bú$_y$-* makes them incompatible with the eventline prefix.

(117) a. *ʔbɨ̀ š-tá= 'ma, š-k-wá= 'šiH ya, ʔbɨ́, dù= 'ʔ*
when EL-SM^1=go EL-F^1-PRG^C=tell now when F^xc^3=come
When I go (there), I'll tell him/her, then, to come (here).

b. *nuya, ya š-kú= 'ʔñɔthe rá$_n$- 'ngų, khà gí= 'cɔ, y*
now now EL-C^2=medicate ST-much ? P^2=feel now

š-ká= 'zɔ
EL-SM^cc^2=recover
Now that you've taken medicine for quite a long time, do you feel that you are getting better?

c. *nù-kí, š-kàn= 'ʔmɨ̀h-ti kár vida mą̂ʔmæto*
xcp EL-SM^cc^I^3=live-AFF xcs3 lifestyle former
But those people, they are just living the way they did before.

d. *hį́ š-kíy= 'hyanti kàr sabe habɨ š-kân= 'ma*
NEG EL-SQ^xc^2=see xcs Isabel where? EL-SM^cc^C^3=go
Didn't you see where Isabel just went?

As in the case of completive prefixes (71b), there are only three prefixes to conjunctively mark action that is not simultaneous with the eventline, and all three are compatible with the eventline prefix. Since the latter denotes an action to be on the eventline or synchronous with it, sequential prefixes denote actions that occur either in the immediate past or in the near future in respect to eventline time. Whether the reference is to past or future time, in reference to that of the speech act, is established by primary prefixes (§3).

(118) a. *ya š-tá= 'koh-kɔ pɨ̀ hâr hwąhį́, khą*
now EL-SM^1=return-1 xc at^s cornfield and C^1=meet-dx
Having just returned from the cornfield, I met him/her.

b. *š-kíy= 'pèni ʔbɨ̀ š-k-wí= 'kòhí*
EL-SQ^xc^2=wash when EL-F^xc^2-PNC^xc=come^back
You will wash it when you come back.

c. *komo bú= 'hwăH kàr karro,*
because SM^xc^3=break^down xcs bus

ya š-kív= 'nšųy dú= 'cə̀hə
now EL-SQ^C^3=become^night C1=arrive^here
Because the bus broke down on the road, it had already become late when we arived here.

As for the occurrence of sequential prefixes with the eventline prefix, the first-person prefix *gà-* (sequential centric first-person) cannot be distinguished phonologically from first-person future-tense *gù-* because it always occurs with a first-order prefix which elides the vowel (§4.2).[15] The first-person excentric prefix *dí-* (sequential excentric first-person) is not

[15]In (119a), the second-order prefix of the second verb, here interpreted as the conjunct prefix *gà-* (sequential centric first-person), might alternatively be interpreted as the primary prefix *gù-* (first-person future).

found with *ší-*. For second person, both *gà$_y$-* (sequential centric$_1$ second-person) and *dí$_y$-* (sequential centric$_2$ second-person), on the other hand, are found with the eventline prefix even in the absence of a first-order prefix, as is the third-person prefix *dí$_v$-* (sequential incompletive third-person).

(119) a. *š-k-rì='planča-gɔ* *š-k-rà='ñą-wi*
EL-SQ^cc^1-DURir^I=iron-1 EL-SQ^cc^1-PNC^ir=talk-di
While I am ironing, you and I can talk.

b. *ʔeš* *š-kà$_y$='hñąši* *nɨr* *thǽgi,* *g-rí$_v$='thoH* *n*
immediate EL-SQ^cc$_1$^2=take cc$_2$s saw F^cc^2-DUR=pass cc$_2$s3

ngų̀ *kàr* *berto*
house xcs Robert
Take the saw right away and go past Robert's house.

c. *ya* *ší-∅='nšųy;* *ʔbɨ̀* *gí='ne* *gì$_y$='ma,* *sta* *ɨ̀r*
now EL-P^3=night when P^2=want F^cc^2=go until ins tomorrow

khą̀ *š-tí$_y$='ma*
and EL-SQ^cc$_2$^2=go
Already it is night; if you want to go, (wait) until tomorrow, and then go.

d. *yɨ̀* *khąʔnį* *mí-∅='ʔəti-hɨ* *mbaškhwa* *cada* *ocho* *día;*
cc$_2$p person IMPF-P^3=do-p fiesta each eight day

š-tí$_v$-='dɔt-hɨ *ɨ̀r* *marte,* *geh* *nɨ̀* *mí-∅='ʔəti-hɨ*
EL-SQ^I^3=touch-p ins Tuesday exist cc$_2$s IMPF-P^3=do-p

mbaškhwa *nɨ́*
fiesta cc$_2$s
These people used to have fiestas once a week; whenever Tuesday came, they would throw a party.

6
First-order Prefixes

First-order prefixes are nonpersonal and aspectual. They always occur together with a primary or a conjunct second-order, person-encoding prefix, and may also occur with a third-order prefix. First-order prefixes are listed in (120) in five subsets which will be discussed in order. Note right away, however, that the fifth set listed in (120e) is anomalous. Its members DO mark person-of-subject. They are further anomalous in not occurring with second-order prefixes and in including two consonants in their phonological form. More on this under the discussion of this subset at the end of this chapter.

(120) a. *rà-* (PNC^ir, punctiliar irrealis, below eye level) §6.1
rá- (PNC^cc, punctiliar centric realis, at eye level) §6.2
bí- (PNC^xc, punctiliar excentric realis, above eye level) §6.3

b. *dì-* (DURir^I, durative irrealis incompletive) §6.4
dì$_V$- (DURir^C, durative irrealis completive) §6.5
rí$_V$- (DUR, durative realis) §6.6

c. *bà-* (PRG^I, progressive incompletive) §6.7
bá- (PRG^C, progressive completive) §6.8

d. *rú-* (FP, future perfect) §6.9

e. *gwà-* (IR^1, first-person irrealis) §6.10
gwìy- (IR^2, second-person irrealis) §6.10

6.1–3 Punctiliar prefixes

The first subset of three prefixes, listed in (120a), mark an action or situation aspectually as PUNCTILIAR—viewed as momentary but without reference to the eventline. They also carry deictic force in relation to the deictic center in various contrasting ways, distinguish realis from irrealis situations, and have special locative functions in definable situations. Details of the use of each prefix are spelled out prefix by prefix in the sections that follow.

6.1. The prefix *rà-* (punctiliar irrealis, below eye level). The primary use of the first prefix of this subset, *rà-* (punctiliar irrealis, below eye level), is to indicate that an action is punctiliar (momentary, viewed perfectively; Comrie 1976:18)—and at deictic center time, without reference to deictic center spatial location. In this use, it occurs only in an irrealis clause, as in (121). Irrealis clauses do not denote specific eventline acts, but rather state indefinite generalities or report projections of what might be.

In (121a), for example, an individual is expected to arrive at a named location at an unknown future time. Although the specific time of arrival is unknown, *rà-* specifies that the inquiry denoted by the second verb will take place immediately upon arrival, which is to say, at deictic center time. Although the phrase *cəti pɨ̀* 'arrive there' specifies motion away from the deictic center, the prefix is neutral on this point. In (121b), no specific going to bed or arising is in focus; but whenever these actions take place, it is implied by the occurrence of *rà-* that a prayer is immediately spoken.

(121) a.

ʔbɨ̀	*∅-rà=ˈcəti*	*pɨ̀*	*hábɨ*	*ʔì=ˈpæH*	*kár*	*ʔñow*
when	P^3-PNC^ir=arrive^there	xc	where?	P^3=work	xcs3	sibling

dàv=ˈñɔ́ni
F^cc^3=inquire

When s/he arrives there where his/her sibling works, s/he will inquire.

b. *kada ʔbɨ d-rà=ˈʔoy, kada ʔbɨ*
each where P^1-PNC^ir=go^to^bed each where

d-rà=ˈnanci, dí=ˈmàʔt ʔòkhą̀
P^1-PNC^ir=get^up P^1=call God
Whenever I go to bed and whenever I get up, I pray to God.

A punctiliar or momentary view of an action is thus expressed in relation to another action whose eventline position is indefinite. This is the force of *rà-* in an irrealis situation and is considered the primary meaning of the prefix.

This same prefix, however, may occur in a realis context with locative force, almost always in the presence of a locative expression in the clause, to direct attention to a location below eye level. In this use, *rà-* (a) only occurs with third-person subjects, (b) may not occur with third-order *mí-* (imperfect), but (c) may occur with the third-order prefix *ší-* (eventline), in which case it actualizes as *nà-*.

(122) a. *kɔti ya kàr za kà ∅-rà=ˈmphɨni*
put! now xcs wood REL P^3-PNC^ir=smoke
Now put that piece of wood that's smoking (down into the fire)!

b. *ya š-∅-nà=ˈʔbən-di wa hâr hɔy nɨr*
now EL-P^3-PNC^ir=lie-just cc₁ at^s ground cc₂s paper
This piece of paper is (just) lying here on the ground.

A third and special use of this irrealis prefix is with verbs of speech, presumably to mark the content of speech acts as other than realis.

(123) a. *ngṵ̌ d-rà=ˈmbe̱n-gɔ, ∅-ˈɨ̀r cí tʔaši ʔye*
as SM^1=PNC^ir=think-1 P^3=be little white rain
I think it is a nice gentle (white) rain.

b. *khą nɨ̀r dohto ya, ∅-rà=ˈma̱n ya, ʔwi̱ti ʔnà-r*
and cc₂s doctor now P^3-PNC^ir=say now toast! one-in little

tɨhki ɨ̀r tʔæy pɨ́
amount ins wheat xc
And the doctor, then, he says, "Toast a little bit of wheat there."

c. *bueno así š-t-rà='mbęni š-t-rà='mbęni ...*
well thus EL-P^1-PNC^ir=think EL-P^1-PNC^ir=think
Well, thus, from time to time I think ...

d. *n-dí='segi-tho nɨm vida, n-d-rà='mąn*
IMPF-P^1=continue-AFF cc₂s1 lifestyle IMPF-SM^1-PNC^ir=say

ya ʔbɨ ... másɨ ∅ ʔbæthri
now when probably inp lie
I kept living in the same way, and I was saying ... probably it was lies.

6.2. The prefix *rá-* (punctiliar centric realis, at eye level). The primary use of the prefix *rá-* is to mark a realis action or situation as punctiliar. It occurs with a wide range of second- and third-order prefixes and normally implies that an action is both temporally and spatially proximate to the deictic center, although a centric$_2$ or excentric adverb in the context may indicate a measure of spatial distance also. Its secondary locative role of indicating action approximately at eye level is difficult to demonstrate since it may be considered the default situation in a locative context. In such a context, lacking a specific reference to a location below or above eye level, *rá-* denotes punctiliar action at eye level. A variety of examples of present-tense forms with all three subject persons are presented in (124).

(124) a. *nùgɔ dí='ʔæn nɨr zæšthi khą̀ nɨr ʔyo ʔì='pa ∅-r*

1 P^1=throw cc₂s sandal and cc₂s dog P^3=go P^3-PNC^cc=bring
I throw this sandal and this dog immediately goes and brings it back.

b. *geʔ kàr ʔbəhñą ką́ d-rá='ʔęh-me ką́*
be xcs vow xcs P^1-PNC^cc=come-px xcs
That is the vow we are now coming (to pay).

c. *d-rá='ma pɨ har tʔɔti xɨtha kàr templo pa gù='khɨši dehe*
P^1-PNC^cc=go xc at^3 well back xcs church so F^1=draw
I'm on my way to the well behind the church house to draw water.

This centric prefix can focus on temporal proximity to the deictic center even though an excentric adverb points to the action taking place somewhat removed spatially from that center, as in (125).

(125) a. *n-d-rá= 'ʔbɨ̀h-ʔbe pɨ̀ ʔmundɔ kàm khwǎ̹dạ*
IMPF-P^1-PNC^cc=be-dx xc Mexico xcs1 brother^of^male
At that time I was there in Mexico City with my brother.

b. *ʔyo dě g-rá= 'kɨti pɨ̀ habɨ Ø-rá= 'ʔbɨ̀H*
NEG! continue P^2-PNC^cc=enter xc where? P^3-PNC^cc=be

kàr sabe
xcs Isabel
Don't be continually going in there where Isabel is.

Without attempting to illustrate all combinations of second-order prefixes with *rá-* (punctiliar centric realis), two nonpresent forms are illustrated in (126). Note in (126b) that although *rá-* has combined with an irrealis prefix, a realis situation is under consideration.

(126) a. *ya g-rá= 'ma pɨ̀ har šų̀mɨy*
now F^1-PNC^cc=go xc at^3 shade
I'm going over there into the shade.

b. *šǐn d_V-rá= 'hų́ wà kàr míši dì$_V$= 'gą́hki nɨ̀r*
if^! SQ^I^3-PNC^cc=sit cc_1 xcs cat P^3-DURir^C=catch cc_2s

cí ngų̌, Ø-dì$_V$= 'zá
small mouse P^3-DURir^C=eat
If only the cat were sitting here so it could catch this little mouse and eat it!

The prefix *rá-* may also combine with either of the two third-order prefixes *mí-* (imperfect) or *ší-* (eventline).

(127) a. *kàm ngų ya habɨ Ø-rá= 'ʔbɨ̀H ya kàr hosé kà*
xcs1 house now where? P^3-PNC^cc=be now xcs José xcs

inez, geʔ pɨ̀ n-d-rá= 'ʔbɨ̀h-kɔ ʔbɨ́
Inez be xc IMPF-P^1-PNC^cc=be-1 when
At my house where José and Inez now live, that's where I lived at that time.

b. *š-tú= 'hanti-ki n-g-rá= 'těš kàr karro pa gwì$_y$= 'ma*
EL-P^1=see-2 IMPF-P^2-PNC^cc=mount xcs bus so IR^2=go

hyaphi
Ixtlahuaca
I saw you getting on the bus to go to Ixtlahuaca.

c. *ʔbɨ̀ n-dí= 'pa pɨ̀, m-∅-rá= 'can-gi*
when IMPF-P^1=go xc IMPF-P^3-PNC^cc=scold-1
When I used to go there, he used to scold me.

(128) a. *ya š-t-rá= 'pɔši kàm ʔwæne, gù= 'mæ-ʔbe*
now EL-P^1-PNC^cc=wrap xcs1 baby F^1=go^d-dx
As soon as I wrap up my baby, we (excl) are going to go.

b. *ya š-k-rá= 'paši*
now EL-P^2-PNC^cc=sweep
You are sweeping (in there).

c. *kár me ∅-rá= 'ʔbæn-tho, gege ya š-∅-ná= 'ngɔni*
xcs3 mother P^3-PNC^cc=lie-AFF ANA now EL-P^3-PNC^cc=move

pɨ̀ hâr gohcibi
xc at^s hearth.
His mother is still lying down. He is moving about at the hearth.

d. *ʔbɨ̀ gwì$_y$= 'ʔño-tho, ya š-k-rá= 'ʔyo pɨ̀ zabi*
when IR^2-walk-AFF now EL-F^xc^2-PNC^cc-walk xc pond

ya, komo gí= 'tihi
now because P^2-walk^fast
If you had walked, by now you would be walking over by the pond, because you walk fast.

e. *nɨ̀r ʔbæhñą ya ší-∅=ndo- 'ndəʔmi kàr karro; ʔbɨ̀*
cc$_2$s woman now EL-P^3=greatly-await xcs bus when

∅-dì$_v$= 'ʔño-tho, ya š-t-rá= 'ʔyo pɨ̀ zabi
P^3-DURir^C^3=walk-AFF now EL-F^xc^3-PNC^cc=walk xc pond
This woman has waited a long time for the bus. If she had walked, she would by now be walking over by the pond.

6.3. The prefix *bí-* (punctiliar excentric realis, above eye level). This prefix contrasts with *rá-* and *rà-* in denoting realis action which is punctiliar, but removed either temporally or spatially from the deictic center. Its excentric reference, away from the deictic center, results in *bí-* never occurring with a first-person-subject prefix, the latter always implying location at the deictic center.

(129) a. *ʔyokạ gy-wí='ʔyo pɨ ʔnẹhẹ, eso š-∅-pá='nza-ki*
why? C^2-PNC^xc=walk xc also that EL-P^3-PRG^C=bite-2
Why did you walk around there, anyway? That's why it bit you.

b. *pa ɨr miercole o jueve, ∅-bí='cɨ hñų̀ semana*
by ins Wednesday or Thursday P^3-PNC^xc=reach three week
By Wednesday or Thursday it will be three weeks.

In contexts where temporal or spatial location is not in view, it figuratively denotes logical distance between two speech acts.

(130) *geʔ kậ ∅-bí='cɨH pɨ kậ*
be xcs P^3-PNC^xc=capture xc xcs
That's what that (utterance) means.

In a locative context, the secondary force of *bí-* is to denote an action located spatially higher than the deictic center, either near to it or far from it.

(131) a. *khà g-wí='ʔbɨ̀h-ke wa ya habɨ ∅-bí='hə kàr*
? P^2-PNC^xc=bc-2 cc_1 now where? P^3-PNC^xc=stand xcs

higante
eucalyptus
Do you live just up here where the eucalyptus tree is growing?

b. *∅-bí=ndo-'po dehe pɨ ñạ*
P^3-PNC^xc=greatly-be water xc above
There is a lot of water up above (on the roof).

c. *Ø-rí$_v$= 'bəš ni Ø-rí$_v$-= 'nkha ni, derečo ni*
P^3-DUR=rise cc$_2$ P^3-DUR=locate cc$_2$ straight cc$_2$ where?

Ø-bí= 'hə nir ndò zǎ
P^3-PNC^xc=stand cc$_2$s great tree
It comes up over there, straight beyond up there (nearby) where that big tree is.

d. *hyanti-hmą Ø-bí= 'təH ni ʔnàr miši*
look!-just P^3-PNC^xc=ride cc$_2$ one^in cat
Look! there's a cat perched up there.

When used with a verb of motion, *bí-* encodes the location of the point of origin.

(132) *bì$_v$= 'ma gá$_n$= 'ngoH pi hár ngų pi habi*
C^3=go SM^cc^C^3=return xc at^3 house xc where?

g$_v$-wí= 'ʔñęhę
SQ^C^3-PNC^xc=come
He returned to his house from whence he had come.

Examples follow of *bí-* occurring with either of the third-order prefixes.

(133) a. *dú= 'hanti-ki-wi n-g-wí= 'ʔyo-wi pi nsan huan*
C^1=see-2-d IMPF-P^2-PNC^xc=walk-d xc San Juan
I saw you two walking around up in San Juan.

b. *pi hâr tʔə, pi san bartolo m-Ø-bí= 'ʔbiH*
xc at^s mountain xc San Bartolo IMPF-P^3-PNC^xc=be one^in

torre kàr tʔə
tower xcs mountain
Up on the hill, in San Bartolo, there was a tower on the hill.

c. *ya š-Ø-pí= 'cəni ni hâr ngų ni*
now EL-P^3-PNC^xc=arrive^there cc$_2$ at^s house cc$_2$

Ø-bí-= 'kha ni
P^3-PNC^xc=locate cc$_2$
Now she is arriving at the house up there (in sight.)

6.4–6 Durative prefixes

The second subset of first-order aspectual prefixes, listed in (120b), mark an action as DURATIVE—as occurring through a span of time, but without reference to the eventline. The first two prefixes in this subset primarily contrast with the third in that the low-tone form occurs in irrealis contexts, the high-tone form in realis contexts.

6.4. The prefix *dì-* (durative irrealis incompletive). This prefix denotes an incompletive and durative action or event that is not specifically factual.

(134) a. *cín g-rì= 'koh-ke ʔbɨ̀ gí= 'pa hyaphi*
early P^2-DURir^I=return-2 when P^2=go Ixtlahuaca
You (customarily) come back early when you go to Ixtlahuaca.

b. *nin te cɨ̀ ∅-dì= 'ʔbɨ̀h-ti-hɨ nɨ́r ngų-hɨ,*
NEG! what? few P^3-DURir^I=be-AFF-p cc_2s3 house-p all

te ʔì= 'pæh-mɨ
what? P^3=work-p
They are hardly ever at home; they do all kinds of work.

c. *hín ge š-k_y-rì= 'kąhki rì ʔyæ*
NEG be EL-F^cc^2-DURir^I=cut^off ins2 hand
Don't be cutting off your hand.

d. *ʔbɨ̀ š-tà$_v$= 'zɨH kàr hñųsną, ya*
when EL-F^cc^3=reach xcs three^months now

š-∅-tì= 'ʔbɨ̀H kwa gege
EL-P^3-DURir^I=be cc_1 ANA
When the three months are up, s/he will (probably) be here.

e. *dí= 'hon-gɔ ʔnàr mɔšte ∅-dì= 'pądi ∅-dì= 'ʔəti*
P^1=seek-1 one^in servant P^3-DURir^I=know P^3-DURir^I=do

hñų́ni
dinner
I'm looking for a maid who would know how to make dinner.

The incompletive irrealis prefix is not much used in present-tense contexts by younger speakers of Otomí, who tend to use future-tense prefixes to express such contingent or potential situations. Thus, the situation expressed in (134e) would more likely be expressed by a younger speaker as in (135).

(135) *dí='hon-gɔ ʔnàr mɔšte dà$_V$='bą̱di dà$_V$='ʔyəti hñų́ni*
P^1=seek-1 one^in servant F^cc^3=know F^cc^3=do dinner
I'm looking for a maid who will know how to make dinner.

Durative irrealis *dì-* may occur with second-order future-tense prefixes. The following conditional sentences have the durative irrealis incompletive prefix *dì-* in protasis, and punctiliar irrealis *rà-* in the apodosis.[15]

(136) a. *ʔbɨ̀ g-rì='ʔbɨ̀h-kɔ wa hám ngų ɨ̀r šųdi, menta*
when F^1-DURir^I=be-1 cc_1 at^1 house ins tomorrow while

g-rà='mpeni, gù='hanti kàr zakhwa
F^1-PNC^ir=wash^clothes F^1=watch xcs pig
If I am here at my house tomorrow, I'll keep an eye on the pig while I am washing clothes.

b. *ʔbɨ̀ g$_y$-rì='ʔbɨ̀H kwa hèr ngų ɨ̀r šųdi,*
when F^cc^2-DURir^I=be cc_1 at^2 house ins tomorrow while

g$_y$-rà='mpeni, gì$_y$='hyanti kàr zakhwa
F^cc^2-PNC^ir=wash^clothes F^cc^2=watch xcs pig
If you are at your house tomorrow, keep an eye on the pig while you are washing clothes.

c. *ʔbɨ̀ dì='ʔbɨ̀H kwà hár ngų ɨ̀r šųdi,*
when F^cc^3^DURir^I=be cc_1 at^3 house ins tomorrow while

d$_V$-rà='mpeni, dà$_V$='hyanti kàr zakhwa
F^cc^3-PNC^ir=wash^clothes F^cc^3=watch xcs pig
If she is here at her house tomorrow, she'll keep an eye on the pig while she is washing clothes.

---

[15]Note in the third-person form, in (136c), that since second-order *dà$_V$-* (F^cc^3) and first-order *dì-* (DURir^I) both begin with *d*, the second-order form is elided entirely, not just the vowel and tone but also the identical consonant *d*. Its presence is thus known only through paradigmatic material of the sort found in (136a)–(136c). As indicated in §1.8, even the augmentative force of *dà$_V$-* (F^cc^3) is blocked by irrealis *dì-* (DURir^I).

The following sentences illustrate the eventline adverb *šì* with imperfect prefix *mí-* and the incompletive durative *dì-*.

(137) a. *ni šì n-g-rì= 'hanti-gɔ-hɨ, khà ya*
NEG! EL IMPF-F^1-DURir^I=watch-1-pi ? now

ší-Ø$_V$= 'thoH kɨ̀ ʔñɔgi
EL-C^3=pass xcp buriers
We (incl) weren't even watching (to see) whether that funeral procession had passed by.

b. *ni šì n-g$_y$-rì= 'hanti-ge-hɨ khà ya*
NEG! EL IMPF-F^cc^2-DURir^I=watch-2-p ? now

mí-Ø= 'thoH kɨ̀ ʔñɔgi[16]
IMPF-P^3=pass xcp buriers
You weren't even watching to see whether that funeral procession was passing by.

c. *nį̀ šì n-Ø-dì= 'hanti nɨ́ ʔnęhę, khà ya*
NEG! EL IMPF-P^3-DURir^I=watch cc$_2$s also ? now

ší-Ø$_V$= 'thoH kɨ̀ ʔñɔgi?
EL-C^3=pass xcp buriers
This person wouldn't even have been watching either (to see) whether that funeral procession had passed by.

d. *ʔbɨ̀ š-tà$_V$= 'zɨH kàr hñųsną, ya*
when EL-F^cc^3=reach xcs three^months now

š-tì= 'ʔbɨ̀H-kwa gege
EL-F^cc^3^DURir^I=be-cc$_1$ ANA
When the three months are up, s/he will probably be here.

[16]There are some utterances which have the unaugmented form of the verb stem after a prefix which calls for stem augment, such as (137b), in which the composite includes *gì$_y$-* (proximal second-person future) but the stem of the verb *'hanti* or *'hyanti* 'watch' occurs in unagumented form, since augmented forms of the verb stem do not appear in irrealis clauses.

e. *š-tá='pæh-kɔ g-rì='panci-gɔ nìm šą̀hį, khą*
EL-SM^1=work-1 SQ^cc^1-DURir^I=roll-1 cc$_2$s1 maguey^fiber and

š-k-rì='ñą-wi
EL-F^1-DURir^I=talk-di
While I work, rolling up my maguey fiber, you and I can talk.

6.5. The prefix *dì$_v$*- (durative irrealis completive). This prefix encodes a completive and durative action or event that is not factual; although anticipated, it did not materialize. In a present-tense context, it encodes a situation known to be contrary-to-fact.

(138) a. *khwá n-dí='ʔɔh-pi okhą nìr mægi ʔñəhə nɨ́*
much IMPF-P^1=request-BEN God cc$_2$s darn! man cc$_2$s

∅-dì$_v$='dù nɨ́, pa gwà='ʔweni, hin gwà='təʔmi-gɔ kár
P^3-DURir^C=die cc$_2$s so IR^1=depart NEG IR^1=await-1 xcs3

genio
disposition
I was very much asking God that this darn man would die, so that I could get away from him. I would not stay around (him with) his (unpleasant) manner.

b. *nùʔbɨ́, cà ∅-dì$_v$='mɔhti-gi*
then really P^3-DURir^C=kill-1
Then he really would have killed me.

c. *ya š-∅-tì$_v$='zəni-hɨ, ʔną́, ya*
now EL-P^3-DURir^C=arrive^there-p say now

š-∅-tì$_v$='zəni-hɨ; má-∅='tų̌ kàr petroleo
EL-P^3^DURir^C=arrive^there-p IMPF-P^3=bring xcs kerosene
They were about to arrive, they said, they were about to arrive; they were bringing that kerosene.

d. *nùʔbɨ ∅-d$_v$='ɨ́r bą̀hci nɨ̀ nɨ́, ∅-dì$_v$='zíš*
if P^3-DURir^C=ins3 child cc$_2$s cc$_2$s P^3-DURir^C=take

hâr dòktór
at^s doctor
If this child were hers, she would take it to the doctor.

6.6. The prefix *rí*$_V$- (durative realis). This prefix encodes action that is durative—or iterative—and disassociated with any deictic reference.

(139) d. *nùwa hį̄ Ø-rí$_V$='nįgi wa, nùpɨ Ø-rí$_V$='nįgi pɨ̌*
cc$_1$ NEG P^3-DUR=appear cc$_1$ xc P^3-DUR=appear xc
Here it doesn't show; on that side it shows.

e. *yǎ Ø-rí$_V$='ʔmɨ̀H nɨ̀ šɨtha hyaphi ką́*
now P^3-DUR=be cc$_2$ back Ixtlahuaca xcs
That one (a town) is over behind Ixtlahuaca.

f. *Ø-rí$_V$='ncɔwi dà$_V$='ʔbɔʔti*
P^3-DUR=fitting F^cc^3=be^killed
He deserves to be killed.

With a momentary verb, the durative prefix may have an iterative force.

(140) *kada n-g$_n$-wá='nzɨ̀ yo kheyæ š-Ø-ní$_V$='ʔmɨ̀h kár*
each IMPF-SM^cc^C^3-PRG^C=reach two year EL-P^3-DUR=be xcs3

ʔñowi
companion
Every time it reached two years, another child was born.

For unknown reasons, perhaps merely morphophonemic, *rí*$_V$- (durative realis) does not occur together with the first-person simultaneous or present-tense prefixes *dá*- or *dí*-. In this context, it is paradigmatically replaced by *rá*- (punctiliar centric realis). Compare the first- and second-person forms in (141a) and (141b). Similarly, in contexts where durative *rí*$_V$- is normally present, the first-person future prefix *gù*- rejects it, with *rá*- appearing instead, as in (141c). There thus seems to be an association between a first-person subject and the centric prefix *rá*-, except when the context includes a motion verb or adverbial element that is less centric than centric$_1$.

(141) a. *d-rá='ma nɨ́*
P^1-PNC^cc=go cc$_2$
I'm going there.

b. *habɨ g-rí$_V$='ma*
where P^2-DUR=go
Where are you going?

c. *ʔì='bìH yìm yæ pa g-rá='pæh-mi*
P^3=be cc$_2$p hand so F^1-PNC^cc=work-p
We (incl) have hands so that we can work.

The durative prefix is frequently found in a nonmotion verb which follows a closely related motion verb. In this context, the durative action tends to be that of the motion verb rather than the action named by the nonmotion verb. The latter is referenced as occurring after the motion has taken place and may not be an action that endures over any significant span of time. In such a context, since motion verbs like 'go' and 'take' denote movement away from the deictic center, the durative verbs marked by *rí$_V$-* are associated with an excentric location.

(142) a. *š-tá=thæš-kɔ š-k-rí$_V$='hehki ní*
EL-SM^1=carry^away-1 EL-F^1-DUR=divide cc$_2$
I will take them and divide them up there.

b. *gù='ma g-rí$_V$='šoh-kɔ nìr templo*
F^1=go F^1-DUR=open-1 cc$_2$s church
I'm going over to open up this church house.

c. *yǎ g$_n$-wá='ʔñę kwa pa d-rí$_V$='ma ʔmundɔ*
now SM^cc^C^3-PRG^C=come cc$_1$ so F^cc^3-DUR=go México
They were coming here on their way to Mexico City.

This prefix may also occur with either of the third-order prefixes.

(143) a. *hín dí='pądi-he há n-g-rí$_V$='ʔño ʔbì*
NEG P^1=know-px how? IMPF-P^2-DUR=walk when

n-g='ír bąhci
IMPF-P^2=be child
We don't know how your life-style was when you were a child.

b. *ʔyɔni ci, hăbi m-∅-rí$_V$='ma ʔbì*
inquire! please where? IMPF-P^3-DUR=go when

m-bú='nthæ-wi kèr ta
IMPF-SM^xc^3=meet-d xcs2 father
Ask him, please, where was he going when he met your father?

c. *gù= 'hą ci nɨ, ya š-k-rí$_V$= 'ma nɨ*
F^xc^2=bring please cc$_2$ now EL-P^2-DUR=go cc$_2$
Please bring me back some, since you're going there.

d. *kàr gonzalez ya š-Ø-ní$_V$= 'ma dù= 'ʔaphi,*
xcs González now EL-P^3-DUR=go F^xc^3=collect^maguey^sap

porke ya ší-Ø$_V$= 'nde
because now EL-C^3=late
Now González is going to go and collect maguey sap, because it's late (afternoon).

e. *bú$_V$= 'ʔęhę š-k-rì$_V$= 'ʔbɨ̀p-hɨ wa*
SM^xc^2=come EL-F^1-DURir^C=be-pi cc$_1$
Come here so that we (incl) can be together here.

f. *š-tù= 'ʔæH kɨ́ ʔnę̌ š-t-rí$_V$= 'goti-hɨ*
EL-F^xc^3=come xcp and EL-F^xc^3-DUR=enclose-p
He will drive them here and put them in jail.

6.7–8 Progressive prefixes

The second subset of first-order prefixes has two members which mark an action as progressive. They are distinguished from each other in that low-tone *bà-* occurs in nonpast or incompletive contexts, whereas high-tone *bá-* occurs in past or completive contexts. With verbs of motion these prefixes indicate action directed inbound, towards the deictic center, in contrast to the use of the durative prefix which in such a context indicates outbound motion away from the deictic center, as discussed above.

6.7. The prefix *bà-* (progressive incompletive). Of the two prefixes in this subset, this is the more restrictive in respect to occurrence with other prefixes. It occurs only with third-person subjects and only with tenses—PRESENT and its close correlate SIMULTANEOUS. Notice that since durative prefixes have a secondary meaning of motion away from the deictic center while progressive prefixes imply motion toward the deictic center, the motion vector at times overrides what would otherwise be a distinction between durative and progressive situations, as in (144a), which represents an iterative rather than truly progressive event. This is also true of (144c).

(144) a. *∅-bà='hæ-gi-tho dá='ʔęhę*
P^3-PRG^I=allow-1-AFF SM^1=come
She allows me to come (here).

b. *š-∅-ní$_{v}$='thogi khą̀ ∅-bà='khɨti kàr nthąhį*
EL-P^3-DUR=pass and P^3-PRG^I=drag xcs rope
He is passing by, and he is (coming) dragging the rope.

c. *ya ší-∅$_{v}$='hñųšadi g$_{n}$-wà='thoH kàr mɔthųhmę*
now EL-C^3=noon SM^cc^I^3-PRG^I=pass xcs bread^seller
It is already noon (midmorning) when the bread seller comes by.

d. *lapi, nin g$_{n}$-wà='ndege!*
pencil NEG! SM^cc^I^3-PRG^I=use^up
Pencils. They (school children) don't even use them up!

Of the two third-order prefixes, this prefix occurs only with *ší-* (eventline).

(145) a. *gege ya š-∅-pà='ʔęH nɨ g$_{n}$-wà='ʔdachæ*
ANA now EL-P^3-PRG^I=come cc$_2$ SM^cc^I^3-PRG^I=alone
She is coming along down there alone.

b. *ya š-∅-pà=ci-'hoH ya*
now EL-P^3-PRG^I=gradual-improve now
Now s/he is gradually getting better.

6.8. The prefix *bá-* (progressive completive). This prefix occurs much more widely with other prefixes than its counterpart *bà-* (progressive incompletive). It may occur, for example, with any of the three persons of subject and with any of three major tense-aspects, with the exception that first-person forms only occur with future tense in association with this prefix.

(146) a. *g-wá='kohi*
F^1-PRG^C=come^back
I'm coming back.

b. *hín g$_{y}$-wá='yoh-mi kèr ta?*
NEG C^2-PRG^C=accompany-d xcs2 father
You were not accompanied by your father?

In (147), the progressive prefix is interpreted as hyperbole to show a close temporal relationship between two events. A man died a short time after he had gotten out of jail, but it is expressed in (147a) as though his exiting the jail was still in progress when he died. Sentence (147b) is similar.

(147) a. *ngų̌ g_n-wá=ˈmbəš husgado, ʔeške $bì_v$=ˈdų́ ní*
as SM^cc^C^3-PRG^C=exit jail EMPH C^3=die cc_2
It seems that no sooner had that one come out of jail than he died.

b. *como ngų̌ š-k_n-wá=ˈnzihi kì dɔʔthi,*
like as EL-SM^cc^C^3-PRG^C=bring xcp sick

š-$kú_y$=ˈʔuni ʔñįthį
EL-C^2=give medicine
As soon as they brought those sick people, you gave them medicine.

This prefix may also occur with either of the third-order prefixes.

(148) a. *ʔbì kha-tho n-g_n-wá=ˈʔñęH kí karta*
when frequent-AFF IMPF-SM^cc^C^3-PRG^C=come xcp3 letter

kàm me, mą́s n-d-rá=ndo-ˈmbęn kàm ngų,
xcs1 mother more IMPF-P^1-PNC^cc=greatly-miss xcs1 house

ʔbí
when
When my mother's letters were coming frequently, I missed my home more (than now).

b. *dú=ˈhanti ʔbì n-g_y-wá=ˈtəh-mi kàr koče nùʔbi*
C^1=see when IMPF-SQ^xc^2-PRG^C=ride-d xcs car when

n-$gú_y$=ˈthoH nìm ngų
IMPF-C^2=pass cc_2s1 house
I saw when you two were riding along in the car, when you passed by my house.

c. *ʔbɨ̀ n-dú='pəH pɨ̀ ham ngų,*
when IMPF-C^1=exit xc at^1 house,

m-∅-bá='ʔą-tho kàm bąhci
IMPF-P^3-PRG^C=sleep-AFF xcs1 child
At the time I came out of my house, my child was sleeping.

d. *dú='hanti-ki ya š-k-wá='ʔę-ke nɨ̀, eso*
C^1=see-2 now EL-SM^cc^2-PRG^C=come-2 cc_2 so

dú='tæn-ki-tho
C^1=follow-2-AFF
I saw that you were coming, so I just followed you here.

e. *š-∅ᵥ-pá='pàh-ki kà š-tá='ʔęhę*
EL-C^3-PRG^C=heat-1 REL EL-SM^1=come
It heated me up as I came.

In its secondary sense of motion towards the deictic center, it can occur in a context where activity away from the deictic center is indicated to imply a later return to the deictic center by the subject. This is illustrated in (146a) above as well as in (149).

(149) *ʔbɨ̀ š-tá='ma, š-k-wá='šiH ya, ʔbɨ̀, dù='ʔ*
when EL-SM^1-go EL-F^1-PRG^C-tell now when F^xc^3-come
When I go (there), I'll tell him/her to come (and then I will return here).

6.9 The future perfect prefix

The future perfect prefix *rú-* always occurs with a second-order future tense prefix to encode future perfect tense. It also always occurs in an eventline clause with third-order prefix *ší-* (eventline) and is semantically incompatible with the third-order prefix *mí-* (imperfect).

(150) a. *ʔbɨ̀ š-k-wí='kohi, ya š-k-rú='khwaʔ-ʔbe*
when EL-F^xc^2-PNC^xc=come^back now EL-F^1-FP=finish-dx

š-k-rú='ci-ʔbe
EL-F^1-FP=eat-dx
When you come back, we two (excl) will have finished eating.

b. *ʔbɨ̀ š-k-wá= 'kohi, ya š-k-rú= 'khwah-mi*
when EL-F^1-PRG^C=come^back now EL-F^cc^2-FP=finish-d

š-k-rú= 'ci-wi
EL-F^cc^2-FP=eat-d
When I come back, you two will have finished eating.

c. *ʔbɨ̀ ya š-t_v-rú= 'ngwadi nɨ̀r ngu̜, š-tá= 'ʔdaš-kɔ,*
when now EL-F^cc^3-FP=finish cc_2s house EL-SM^1=move-1 when
When this house is [will have been] finished, I will then move here.

In the apodosis of a negative condition, a verb with *rú-* and its accompanying future-tense prefix completes a contrary-to-fact condition.

(151) a. *ʔbɨ̀ ∅-dɨ̀$_v$= 'hi̜ná̜ nɨ̀m ngu̜, ya š-k-rú= 'tɔy*
when P^3-IR^C^3=not^be cc_2s1 house now EL-F^1-FP=buy
If it were not for my house (which I'm building), I would have already bought it.

b. *ʔbɨ̀ hín gwɨ̀$_y$= 'ma rì ngu̜, ya š-k_y-rú= 'pa̜di*
when NEG IR^2=go in2 house now EL-F^cc^2-FP=know

∅=rá$_n$- 'zɔ
P^3=ST-good
If you hadn't gone to your house (country), by now you would have known (our language) well.

c. *ʔbɨ̀ hín dɨ̀$_v$= 'ʔwa̜y, ya pé*
when NEG EL-C^3^DURir^C-FP=rain now probably

š-t_v-rú=ci- 'hwiš nɨ̀r hwa̜hi̜
EL-F^cc^3-FP=little-dry cc_2s cornfield
If it hadn't rained, this cornfield would probably have dried out somewhat.

Sentence (152) illustrates a contrary-to-fact condition in which the future perfect verb is embedded within the noun phrase subject of a sentence whose predicator is the negative word *hín*.

(152) *hį́ í bą̀hci-gi-he tema ʔñəhə š-tᵥ-rû='ʔyəte kà*
NEG inp3 child-1-px in man EL-F^cc^3-FP=do REL

∅=rấₙ-'ncʔo
P^3=ST-evil
We (excl) are not the offspring of some man who would have done evil.

Where we might expect *rà-* with the third-person present-tense prefix in an eventline verb *(ší- + ∅ + rà-),* the proximal third-person simultaneous present-tense prefix *gàₙ-* seems to be the prefix of choice.

(153) *ʔì='mą̄n nɨ̀r bą̀hci, ʔbɨ̀ ʔì='pəni yǎnɨ,*
P^3=say cc₂s child when P^3=go^out far

š-kàₙ='nzəhə, ∅-bà='həši chąši
EL-SM^cc^I^3=arrive^here P^3-PRG^I=erupt rash
This child says, when he goes far away and arrives back, he breaks out in a rash.

6.10 Person-marking irrealis prefixes

As indicated at the beginning of this chapter, the two prefixes in this subset are anomalous in several ways. They mark person-of-subject, they fail to occur with second-order prefixes (which normally mark person-of-subject), and they have a CCV phonological structure, which is normal for a string of two prefixes but not for single prefixes. These anomalies are accounted for if these prefixes are considered to be fused forms based on a second-order and a third-order prefix. Unfortunately, there does not seem to be a straightforward way to choose sequences of the prefixes described heretofore which, would yield the meanings these fused forms have. For this reason, they are treated here as units, but acknowledging the probability that they are etymologically complex.

The two forms encode contingent or potential situations which are nonfactual at deictic-center time, as in (154). As unrealized events, location in respect to the deictic center is irrelevant and unmarked. Note incidentally in (154a) that the durative irrealis prefix occurs with a noun phrase as predicate, the indefinite first-person possessed determiner fusing phonologically with the prefix *(dì- + ɨ̀m > dɨ̀m).*

(154) a. *nùʔbɨ dìm bą̀hci-gɔ nɨ́, gwà='ciš hâr doktor*
when DURir^I^1 child-1 cc₂s IR^1=take at^s doctor
If this were my child, I would take him/her to the doctor.

b. *dí='ʔį̨n-gɔ gwìy='ʔdah-ki cɨ ɨ̀r ʔñį̨thį̨*
P^1=say-1 IR^2=give-1 little ins medicine
I think you could give me a little bit of medicine.

In both completive and incompletive contexts, irrealis prefixes express unrealized or frustrated situations intended or hoped for at deictic center time or at a time prior to deictic center time, but which are contrary-to-fact.

(155) a. *š-tá='tų̨ʔti-he kɨ̀m wade-he gwà='mɔh-me hyaphi, khą̨*
EL-SM^1=tie-px xcp1 chicken-px IR^1=go^p-px Ixtlahuaca and

gwà='ciš-he ʔnàr zakhwa
IR^1=take-px one^in pig
We had tied (the legs of) our chickens; our (unfulfilled) intention being to go to Ixtlahuaca and to take a pig.

b. *ʔbɨ̀ gwìy='ʔño-tho, ya š-k-rá='ʔyo pɨ̀ zabi*
when IR^2=walk-AFF now EL-F^xc^2-PNC^cc-walk xc pond

ya, como gí='tihi
now because P^2=walk^fast
If you had walked, you would now be walking over by the pond, because you walk fast.

The occurrence of these irrealis prefixes with the eventline prefix is illustrated in (156).

(156) a. *ya digeʔbɨ ya, dú='hnìni ya, ya š-kwà='tų̨*
now then now C^1=ill now now EL-IR^1=die
Then after that I got ill and was about to die.

b. *mą̂-šųdi habɨ š-kwì$_y$='ʔño, hǎbɨ š-kwì$_y$='nanci,*
this-morning where? EL-IR^2=walk where? EL-IR^2=arise

m-∅=rá$_n$-ndò-'ncæ
IMPF-P^3=ST-greatly-cold

This morning, wherever you might walk, wherever you might get up, it was very cold.

7
Otomí Text

In this final chapter, a short Otomí text is presented, according to the analysis presented in preceding chapters, to illustrate a more extended discourse than the preceding discussion has allowed. This text was originally given to me informally by my language associate, Sabina Pimeño de Morales, and is an account of a true incident. At my request, she repeated the account for me to record on a cassette. Her second rendition, however, lacked some of the details which she had included in her original, informal account. So I reminded her of those details and asked her to repeat part of the story again, including those details. Sentences (157) through (162) are from the first recording; (163) through the final sentence are from the second. It is for this reason that sentences (163) and (164) each have different third-person subjects and that there is no indication at the beginning of (164) that its subject is the same as that of (162) but different from that of (163). Had the text been given without emendation, either the noun phrase 'the mule of Cesario's family' or possibly an independent anaphoric pronoun would have been used at the beginning of (164).

(157)	*nɨ̀r*	*kwento*	*dige*	*kàr*	*phɨ̌nci,*	*hà*	*dá='phɨ̌nci,*	*té*
	cc$_2$s	story	about	xcs	fall	how?	SM^1=fall	what?

	dú='kha-he,	*há*	*gá$_n$='ʔyenti-gi*	*nɨ̀m*	*phani-he.*
	C^1=do-px	how	SM^cc^I^3=knock^down-1	cc$_2$s1	horse-px

This is the story of the fall, how I fell, what we did, how our horse knocked me down.

(158) *n-dí='mpɔh-me gwà='mɔh-me hyaphi mą́-nonši.*
IMPF-P^1=happy-px IR^1=go-px Ixtlahuaca former-Monday
We were happy that we were going to Ixtlahuaca last Monday.

(159) *nùya š-tá='tų?ti-he kɨ̀m wade-he gwà='mɔh-me hyaphi,*
now EL-SM^1=tie-px xcp1 chicken-px IR^1=go-px Ixtlahuaca

khą̀ gwà='ciš-he ?nàr zakhwa.
and IR^1=take^along-px one^in pig
We had tied the legs of our chickens, we were going to go to Ixtlahuaca and we were going to take along a pig.

(160) *khwá n-dí='šəni-he*
much IMPF-P^1=hurry-px
We were hurrying very much.

(161) *dige ?bɨ́ dú='pəni-he, n-dí='?bɔp-he nɨ̀ thí, hín*
so then C^1=go^out-px IMPF-C^1=stand-px cc_2 outside NEG

té n-dí='mbę́ni-he.
what? IMPF-C^1=think-px
So then we went out of the house; we were standing out in the yard; we were not worrying about anything.

(162) *?nę̌ bú=?nà-'k?ą̀ ya kár mačo kí sario,*
but SM^xc^3=suddenly-appear now xcs3 mule xcp3 Cesario

bú='k?ą̀ nɨ̀ hâr zaphani, m-bá=ndo-'timphani,
SM^xc^3=appear cc_2 at^s cornstalk IMPF-PRG^C=greatly-gallop

m-bá='cų kɨ̀ ?yó.
IMPF-PRG^C=fear xcp dog
But then suddenly the mule of Cesario's family appeared; he appeared over there among the cornstalks; he was galloping fast; he was afraid of the dogs.

(163) *∅-bà=ndò='khošini kɨ̀ zaphani gₙ-wà='ʔñę̌ʔ*
P^3-PRG^I=greatly-rustle xcp cornstalk SM^cc^3-PRG^I=come

kɨ̀ ʔyo, khą̀ ∅-bà='phəge.
xcp dog and P^3-PRG^I=bark
There is a lot of rustling in the cornstalks as the dogs come, and they come along barking.

(164) *bú='thoh nɨ̀ hábɨ̀ ∅-rà=ʔbɨ̀h nɨ̀m phani-he, bú*
SM^xc^3=pass cc_2 where P^3-PNC^ir=be cc_2s1 horse-px SM^xc^3 cc_2

m-∅-bá=ndo-timphani m-∅-bá=ncų
IMPF-P^3-PRG^C=greatly-gallop IMPF-P^3-PRG^C=fear
He passed by there where our horse is; he passed by there galloping fast; he was very frightened.

(165) *pé bú='ncų ya nɨ̀m phani-he, bú='kʔóš kàr*
again SM^xc^3=fear now cc_2s1 horse-px SM^xc^3=pull^up xcs

estaka m-ríᵥ=ʔn-'ą́ʔmi.
stake IMPF-DUR=PASS-tether
Our horse also got frightened; he pulled up the stake to which he was tethered.

(166) *bú=ndò-'timphani ya nɨ́, biᵥ='thoh-ti wa hábɨ̀*
SM^xc^3=greatly-gallop now cc_2s C^3=pass-AFF cc_1 where

n-dí='ʔbɔp-he hâr thí.
IMPF-P^1=stand-px at^s yard
He galloped fast; he passed by right here where we were standing in the yard.

(167) *bìᵥ='thoh-ti wa hâr thí, ya š-tìᵥ='zɨ̀hti nɨ̀*
C^3=pass-AFF cc_1 at^s yard now EL-DURir^C=catch cc_2s Abel

dìᵥ='zɔci.
DURir^C=trample
He passed by here in the yard; he was about to run into Abel and trample him.

(168) *eso, dú='cɔ dú='pih ya ʔbɨ́, mą̂s š-∅-tìᵥ*
so C^1=try C^1=frighten now then hoping EL-P^3-DURir^C=stand

o d-ríᵥ='mą̌ nɨ̀ ∅-ríᵥ='nkha nɨ́.
or DURir^C-DUR=go cc₂ P^3-DUR=located cc₂
And so I tried to frighten him away, hoping that he would stand still or go around on the other side.

(169) *hín gáₙ='ne gáₙ='ʔmɔy, š-∅-níᵥ='thogi, khą̀*
NEG SM^cc^3=^want SM^cc^3=stand EL-P^3-DUR=pass and

∅-bà='khɨ̀ti kàr nthą̌hį, khą̌ ʔì='tų̌-di kàr estaka.
P^3-PRG^I=drag xcs rope and P^3=carry-AFF xcs stake
He would not stop; he goes zooming by; he is dragging the rope; it has the stake still tied to it.

(170) *š-∅-níᵥ='mpɔti kàr nthą̌hį nɨ̀m wá.*
EL-P^3-DUR=wrap xcs rope cc₂s1 leg
The rope is wrapping itself around my leg.

(171) *d-rá='phɨnci, ʔbɨ́, m-∅-ríᵥ='duš-ki, ʔbɨ́,*
P^1-PNC^cc=fall^down then IMPF-P^3-DUR=carry^away-1 then

gíᵥ='mæ-gi hâr tʔɔti.
SQ^C^3=lay-1 at^s well
I fall down, then; he is dragging me along, then; and then he leaves me by the well.

(172) *pe dí='ʔį̌n-gɔ hábɨ̀ kɨtʔa metro wǎ hábɨ̀ ʔdahto*
probably P^1=say-1 where? five meter or six that

gáₙ='duš-ki, ya gíₙ='yæn-gi hâr tʔɔti.
SM^C^3=carry^away-1 now SQ^C^3=throw^down-1 at^s well
I would say it was probably around five or six meters that it dragged me along and then threw me down at the well.

(173) *mí-∅='bɔh ya nɨ̀m ta-he, bìᵥ='maʔti ∅-dìᵥ='ʔmɔy.*
IMPF-P^3=stand now cc₂s1 father-px C^3=call P^3-DURir^C=stand
My husband (*lit.* our father) was standing there; he called to it to stand still.

(174) *bì*$_v$*='mă gí*$_v$*='ʔmɔ hâr thi.*
C^3=go SQ^C^3=stand at^s yard
And it went and stood in the yard.

(175) *dú='ką̂ʔmi ya kàr nthą̆hį nɨ̀m wá, š-∅-kí*$_v$*=ndò-'mpɔti*
C^1=take^off now xcs rope cc$_2$s1 leg EL-SQ^C^3=greatly-wrap

khą̀ š-∅-kí$_v$*=ndò-'hyǽti.*
and EL-P^3-SQ^C^3=greatly-cut^into
Then I took the rope off of my leg; it had wound around it a lot and had cut into it.

(176) *dú='ʔbɔʔ pɨ ya, nkháʔmɨ hín té n-dí='senti.*
C^1=stand xc now seems NEG what? IMPF-P^1=feel
Then I stood up; it seemed as though I did not feel any pain.

(177) *∅=cí-'yă ya ką́, ya š-tí='senti*
P^3=small-long^time now xcs now EL-P^1=feel

∅-rá=ndò-'ɨ nɨ̀m šĭnthe, stà ngų̆ ya hín
P^3-PNC^cc=greatly-hurt cc$_2$s1 thigh almost like now NEG

gwà='hɔti kà ∅-rá='ɨ́ nɨ̀m šĭnthe, ya
IR^1=endure REL P^3-PNC^cc=hurt cc$_2$1s thigh now

š-∅-ná=ndò=ngų ∅-rá=ʔɨ́.
EL-P^3-PNC^cc=greatly-much P^3-PNC^cc=hurt
Quite a little while after that, then, I felt my thigh hurt an awful lot; it was almost as though I could not bear the amount that my thigh hurt; by then it hurt an awful lot.

(178) *dige ʔbɨ ya, dú='keha-bi-he kà tó ɨr mæhti*
so then now C^1=complain-BEN-px REL who? ins3 possession

kàr mačo.
xcs mule
So then we complained to the person to whom the mule belongs.

(179) *dà$_{v}$='ʔyəthe-gi, komo geʔ kár ncʔohki kà*
F^cc^3=treat^medically-1 because be xcs3 fault REL

š-∅-pá='piH kàm phani-he
EL-P^3-PRG^C=frighten xcs1 horse-px
He should pay for my treatment, because it is his fault that our horse got frightened.

(180) *bì$_{v}$='hñą mà'dé kàr ndą̀-ntʔəthe.*
C^3=take half xcs cost-treatment
He paid for half of the medical treatment.

(181) *eške dú='ma nɨ hâr mediko, š-∅-pá='ʔdah-ki*
immediately C^1=go cc$_2$ at^s doctor EL-P^3-PRG^C=give-1 xcp

poyeta ko kɨ̀ pastilya.
injection and xcp pill
Right away I went to the doctor; he gave me injections and pills.

(182) *ngų̌ ší-∅='hehke mà'dé kár ʔɨ kàr golpe dú='thogi.*
seems EL-P^3=divide half xcs3 pain xcs blow C^1=pass
It seems as though they have considerably reduced the pain of the injury I suffered.

(183) *ʔì='cʔæ̀ pɨ kàr ʔbède ką́.*
P^3=end xc xcs account xcs
That story finishes there.

Index

H

I

M

N

P

Q

R

S

T

V

www.ingramcontent.com/pod-product-compliance
Lightning Source LLC
LaVergne TN
LVHW020645100826
845148LV00012B/2344

* 9 7 8 0 8 8 3 1 2 6 0 5 9 *